BOOK TITLE

THE KINGDOM FIGHT

IBN ALI

BOOK TITLE

Copyright © 2025 Ibn Ali
All rights reserved.

ISBN: 978-1-957815-12-1 Paperback
ISBN: 978-1-957815-13-8 Hardback

Introduction to "The Kingdom Fight"

By Rahaman Ali

With great pride and profound love, I write this introduction to "The Kingdom Fight," a book that serves as a personal journey and a tribute to my brother, Muhammad Ali. Reflecting on Muhammad's legacy, I have most profound admiration for how my son, Ibn, has honored that legacy through his transformative journey over these 40 days. This book is a testament to Ibn's physical and spiritual growth and reflects Muhammad's wisdom, discipline, and unwavering faith.

Growing up with Muhammad, I witnessed firsthand the battles he fought in the ring and in life. He was more than just a champion; he was a beacon of hope, a voice for the voiceless, and a symbol of resilience. Muhammad's strength wasn't just in his fists but in his spirit. He believed that true greatness came from within, from a deep connection to God and a commitment to serving others.

As I read "The Kingdom Fight," I couldn't help but hear my brother's voice in every chapter. His quotes, woven throughout the narrative, are more than just words; they embody his philosophy on life. Muhammad believed in the power of the mind, the importance of discipline, and the necessity of faith. He often said, "Service to others is the rent you pay for your room here on earth," a principle that guided his every action. Ibn, you have taken these teachings to heart and transformed them into a journey that honors Muhammad and inspires others to find their path to greatness.

If Muhammad were here today, he would be immensely proud of your work, Ibn. He would see in you the same fire that burned within him, the same unyielding determination to rise above challenges and become the best version of yourself. As he did so many times, he would remind you, "It isn't the mountains ahead to climb that wear you out; it's the pebble in your shoe." And he would be thrilled to see how you have removed those pebbles, one by one, to clear the path for your journey.

Muhammad's legacy is one of courage, faith, and relentless pursuit of excellence. "The Kingdom Fight" captures this essence beautifully. It is a book that not only chronicles your transformation, Ibn, but also serves as a guide for anyone seeking to embark on their journey of self-discovery and growth. You have used Muhammad's words as both a compass and a sword, navigating the challenges and fighting the battles that have led you to this moment.

Ultimately, "The Kingdom Fight" is not just your story, Ibn—it is a continuation of Muhammad's legacy. It reminds us that our greatest fights are not against others but within ourselves. In these internal battles, we discover our true strength and purpose. As your father, I am proud of the man you have become, and as Muhammad's brother, I know he would be proud, too.

May this book inspire others to find their strength, fight their battles, and live their lives with the same courage and conviction Muhammad did. And may it remind us all that, like Muhammad, we too can change the world—one step, one fight, one victory at a time.

BOOK TITLE

Some time ago, my dear friend, Pastor Bernadette Smith, invited me to an event in Michigan. The event was to include a speech by the nephew of the Great One - Muhammad Ali. As someone who has been involved with the fighting arts for the majority of my life, I was excited to attend.

The event was terrific, but Ibn Ali truly stood out. I was surprised that the champion boxer nephew of the original GOAT was a Christian pastor, an articulate speaker, and a generally inspiring individual. Ibn was unapologetic about his faith, uncharacteristically humble, and simply someone who wanted to serve God.

We spent a fair bit of time chatting that day and became fast friends. Since that time, I have been honored to stand with Ibn in launching and developing a ministry. His singular focus on standing in the word of Christ and bringing that word to as many people as possible is inspiring. At the same time, his willingness to understand the broken nature of man and to stand by those who are broken as Christ did is a trait I wish more people had.

It is my great honor to call Ibn a friend, and I have a sincere hope that his work on these pages and in the ministry will facilitate the good he hopes to bring to the world.

Thomas Renz

Renz Law, LLC
419-351-4248
www.renz-law.com

ACKNOWLEDGMENTS

To Elohim, the Almighty, my Creator and Sustainer—thank You. This book is a testament to Your boundless power to transform lives, renew minds, and awaken souls to their divine purpose. Through Your grace, I write, through Your Spirit, that I am strengthened, and through Your truth that I stand.

To my family, the lineage that grounds me. To my father, for his steadfast faith and unwavering belief in me, and to my mother, whose quiet strength reflects grace in its purest form. To my uncle, Muhammad Ali, whose life displayed courage and conviction, teaching the world that greatness is measured by faith, compassion, and resilience. While I am honored to carry forward his legacy, I walk first and foremost in the calling of Yeshua, the Christ, whose purpose transcends earthly fame and whose love knows no bounds.

To the mighty men and women of faith—the generals of God—who have paved the way and shaped the ecclesia into a force for the Kingdom. To Dr. Myles Munroe, whose revelations on purpose and the Kingdom forever transformed my understanding of identity and calling. To R.W. Schambach, whose boldness in proclaiming the miraculous reminded me that nothing is impossible with God. To A.A. Allen and Lester Sumrall, who moved with power and authority, teaching me that faith is an unshakable force against any darkness. Their lives and ministries stand as beacons, lighting the path for those of us called to walk in faith and fearless devotion.

To you, the reader—the warrior of faith, the seeker of truth—this book is for you. The 40-Day Transformation is not just a book but a journey into the heart of God's purpose for your life. It is written for those who are ready to rise in strength, live in purpose, and become flames of hope in a world that yearns for light. I am humbled to walk this path with you, knowing that Elohim leads us both in His mighty hand.

And finally, to the unsung heroes—editors, friends, and believers who worked behind the scenes to bring this vision to life. Your dedication and faith have helped create something more than words on a page; this is a call to action, a mission to ignite transformation, and a movement that stands on the foundation of the Kingdom. May these words uplift, inspire, and empower you to walk in faith, live with passion, and transform the world through the love of Yeshua, the Christ. This is a call to rise—to purpose, destiny, and greatness.

With all honor and reverence,
Ibn Ali

BOOK TITLE

CONTENTS

Page 10	Introduction: Carrying Forward the Torch of Faith and Resilience
	Week 1: Setting the Foundation
Page 13	Day 1: Identify the Change You Want to Make
Page 22	Day 2: Understand Your Why
Page 28	Day 3: Set Clear, Achievable Goals
Page 36	Day 4: Visualize Success
Page 43	Day 5: Create a Plan
Page 48	Day 6: Build a Support System
Page 55	Day 7: Rest and Reflect
	Week 2: Building Momentum
Page 62	Day 8: Start Small
Page 69	Day 9: Establish Routines
Page 75	Day 10: Track Your Progress
Page 82	Day 11: Overcome Mental Barriers
Page 89	Day 12: Stay Focused
Page 95	Day 13: Embrace Challenges
Page 102	Day 14: The Will and The Skill
	Week 3: Deepening the Commitment
Page 108	Day 15: The Power of Silence
Page 113	Day 16: Practice Discipline
Page 118	Day 17: Adjust Your Plan
Page 124	Day 18: Seek Inspiration
Page 131	Day 19: Overcome Fear
Page 138	Day 20: Strengthen Your Support System
Page 143	Day 21: Rest and Reflect

	Week 4: Solidifying the Change
Page 148	Day 22: Embrace the New You
Page 154	Day 23: Keep Going
Page 161	Day 24: Measure Your Success
Page 167	Day 25: Rest but Never Quit
Page 173	Day 26: Title: The Race of Faith
Page 178	Day 27: Refine Your Goals
Page 184	Day 28: The Will to Win
	Week 5: Achieving and Sustaining Change
Page 190	Day29: Title: The Path of Service
Page 195	Day 30: The Path to Triumph
Page 200	Day 31: The Journey to Recognizing Your Unique Worth
Page 205	Day 32: Maintain Balance
Page 210	Day 33: Reflect on the Journey
Page 218	Day 34: A Journey to Joy
Page 223	Day 35: Striving for Greatness
	Week 6: Finish Strong
Page 228	Day 36: A Journey of Identity and Strength
Page 234	Day 37: Believing in the Possible
Page 239	Day 38: The Gift of Friendship
Page 245	Day 39: Mapping Change
Page 250	Day 40: Help People
Page 255	Conclusion
Page 257	Ministry Websites

Introduction: Carrying Forward the Torch of Faith and Resilience

I dedicate this book to my Uncle Muhammad Ali and the spiritual influence of Momma Bird, Odessa Grady Clay.

This book aims to inspire greatness through faith, resilience, and the timeless wisdom of Muhammad Ali's quotes, intertwined with biblical references; it also honors the legacy of spiritual and moral guidance passed down through generations.

To the enduring legacy of my uncle, Muhammad Ali, and the spiritual guidance of my grandmother, Momma Bird (Odessa Grady Clay):

While Poppa Cassius Clay Sr. was known for his wit and penchant for rhyme, it was Odessa Grady Clay, affectionately referred to as "Momma Bird," who instilled spiritual depth and growth in both her sons, including my uncle Muhammad Ali (formerly known as Cassius Clay Jr.) and my father, Rahman Ali (formerly Rudolph Valentino Clay). She was the pillar of spiritual guidance in the family, regularly taking them to church and nurturing their faith. Poppa Cassius Sr., on the other hand, faced personal battles with alcohol and relationships, contrasting with the spiritual foundation Momma Bird aimed to provide for their family.

Momma Bird was more than just a woman of faith; she was a beacon of light whose life was a testament to the power of belief and the strength of character. She instilled in our family the values of persistence. Poppa Cassius Sr. highlighted the importance of one's spiritual journey by providing the irreplaceable gift of humor to navigate life's tumultuous seas with wit and grit. It was from this rich soil that Uncle Muhammad's gifts flourished, capturing the world's imagination not just with his prowess in the ring but with his quick wit and profound insights into life's more significant battles.

Today, I stand as a bearer of this legacy, carrying forward the gift bestowed upon us. It is a legacy not of mere physical strength but of the indomitable spirit that defines true greatness. My Uncle Muhammad, with his life, taught us that the battles fought in the silence of one's heart are as significant as those fought under the glaring lights of the world stage.

This book is a tribute to the legacy of my uncle and the deep spiritual foundation my grandfather and grandmother laid. It is a call to all who read these words to pursue the greatness that God has placed within them. For, as it was said, "I knew you before you were in your mother's womb." This divine knowledge speaks of a purpose and destiny woven into the very fabric of our being, a call to greatness that transcends the physical and touches the essence of who we are meant to be.

May the journey through these pages ignite in you the same fire that blazed in my uncle's heart. May it inspire you to climb mountains, face giants, and discover the champion within. For in each of us lies an untapped reservoir of potential, a spark waiting to be kindled into a flame that can light the world.

To the legacy of Muhammad Ali, may these words be a bridge for future generations to cross, carrying forward the torch of faith, resilience, and the relentless pursuit of greatness.

Week 1: Setting the Foundation

Day 1: Identify the Change You Want to Make

Ali's Quote: *"The man who has no imagination has no wings."*

Scripture: *"Where there is no vision, the people perish: but he that keepeth the law, happy is he."* - Proverbs 29:18

Prayer: Heavenly Father, give the reader a clear vision for their life. May they see the possibilities and let Your wisdom fuel their imagination. Amen.

Setting the Foundation My First Breath

Prayer: Heavenly Father, give the reader a clear vision for their life. May they see the possibilities and let Your wisdom fuel their imagination. Amen.

Setting the Foundation My First Breath.

The battle for my soul began before I even took my first breath. My father was the first to declare it. He held me high above his head the moment I was born, his voice booming through the small hospital room, "Allahu Akbar!" The words echoed off the sterile walls, a declaration of my identity before I could form one for myself.

But something else was happening in that room as I dangled in my father's hands. My mother, weak and exhausted from the hours of labor, lay in her hospital bed. Her voice, though softer, was no less resolute. "No," she whispered, her eyes locked on mine, "he belongs to Jesus."

In that moment, I became the object of a spiritual tug-of-war. My father, a devout Muslim, was eager to see me follow in his footsteps, to raise me in the faith that had defined his life. But my mother had other plans set in motion long before I entered this world.

She told me later that the battle for my soul had begun even before the doctors confirmed her pregnancy. One night, as she prayed, she felt the presence of the Holy Spirit so powerfully that it brought her to tears. She heard His voice clearly: "You are pregnant. It's a boy. He will be a mouthpiece for My kingdom."

From that moment on, my mother dedicated me to Jesus. She prayed over me daily, even when I was just a flutter in her womb, believing with all her heart that I was destined for something greater than either of us could comprehend.

Growing up, I felt the weight of these conflicting expectations. Every morning, as the first light of dawn filtered through the curtains, my father would wake me for prayer. I would kneel beside him, reciting the words of the Quran I had learned, while inside, a quiet storm raged. I was torn between the teachings of my father and the whispers of my mother, whispers that told me of a different God, a God of love and grace, a God who had claimed me before I even knew what it meant to belong.

My father was a man of tradition and strength; his expectations were like chains around my soul. He shaped much of my early identity, and I feared disappointing him more than anything else. I wanted to make him proud, to be the son he envisioned, but something inside me yearned for more—something that whispered that I was meant for a different path.

As I grew older, that whisper became harder to ignore. My mother had shared stories of Jesus with me in secret, stories that resonated with something deep inside of me. She would tell me about His love, His sacrifice, and His promise of eternal life. These stories painted a picture of a God who wasn't distant and demanding but close and compassionate. The Jesus she spoke of was a God who knew me, had plans for me, and called me His own long before I was born.

But with every story she told, the tension in my heart grew. I felt caught between two worlds—one built on my father's traditions and expectations and another rooted in the love and grace of Jesus Christ. I didn't know how to reconcile the two, and the fear of what it might mean to choose one over the other consumed me.

For years, I kept up the facade. I would join my father in prayer each day, my lips moving, but my heart disengaged. I felt like a fraud, living a life that wasn't mine. The words I recited felt hollow, like they belonged to someone else, not me. I was living in a shadow, afraid to step into the light of the truth that was growing inside of me.

Then, one night, everything changed. I was lying in bed, staring at the ceiling, when the weight of it all became too much to bear. Tears streamed down my face as I silently cried out, not to Allah, but to Jesus—the Jesus my mother had introduced me to. "Jesus," I whispered, "I don't know what to do. I'm so scared. Please, help me."

As I prayed, a sense of peace began to wash over me, a peace I had never known before. It was as if Jesus Himself was there in the room with me, whispering words of comfort and strength into my heart. "You are mine," I felt Him say. "Do not be afraid. I will give you the courage to be who you are meant to be."

As the sun began its slow ascent the following morning, I joined my father in prayer. But this time, I couldn't recite the familiar words. I stood there in silence, my hands trembling, my heart pounding in my chest.

"Ibn," my father's voice cut through the silence, "why aren't you praying?"

I looked up at him, tears filling my eyes. "Father," I said, my voice shaking, "I can't do this anymore. I can't pray to Allah. I believe in Jesus."

The silence that followed was suffocating. I watched as my father's face contorted in confusion and anger. "What are you saying? You're betraying everything we stand for, everything I've taught you!"

"I know," I whispered, my heart breaking at the pain in his eyes. "But I can't deny what I believe. Jesus is the way."

His hand twitched as if he might strike me, but he didn't. Instead, he turned away, unable to look at me. "You've brought shame to this family," he muttered, his voice filled with a sadness that cut me to the core.

I wanted to run to him and tell him I was still his son and loved him, but I couldn't. I had to stand firm. I had to be brave.

That night, for the first time in my life, I knelt alone in prayer. But this time, it wasn't out of fear or obligation. It was out of love, a deep conviction that had been growing within me for years. I prayed for my father that one day he might come to know the truth that had set me free. As I prayed, I felt a peace wash over me, a peace that came from knowing that I had finally faced my greatest fear and had found the courage to be true to who I was meant to be.

The battle for my soul had been fierce, but it had also been won—by the One who had claimed me before I took my first breath. The words of Muhammad Ali echoed in my mind, "I know where I'm going, and I know the truth, and I don't have to be what you want me to be. I'm free to be what I want."

At that moment, I knew that the expectations of others no longer bound me. I was free—free to be the person God had created me to be, free to walk the path He had laid out for me, and free to live my life for Him, no matter what the cost.

Prophetic Word on Identifying Change

The Lord is stirring within you a desire for transformation, a longing to see change in your life that aligns with His perfect will. I hear the Lord saying, "This is a time of new beginnings, a season where I give you the vision and the imagination to see beyond your current circumstances. I am placing within you the wings to soar into the destiny I have prepared for you."

God encourages you to be bold in identifying the change you want to make. "Do not limit yourself," says the Lord, "for I am the God of the impossible. What you can envision, I can bring to pass. Allow your imagination to be fueled by My wisdom and My Spirit, and you will see doors open that you never thought possible."

As you write down the specific change you want to make, the Lord reminds you that clarity is critical. "Where there is no vision, the people perish," he says. "But when you have a clear vision, guided by My Word, you will find the direction and purpose that leads to true fulfillment."

The Lord is with you as you take this first step. "Trust in My guidance," he says. "I am giving you a vision that is not just for today but for your future. Embrace it, write it down, and watch as I begin to bring it to life."

You are not alone in this journey—God is with you, guiding each step and providing the wisdom you need. This moment is your first step into His vision for you, your first step toward embracing the change you desire and moving forward confidently in His plan.

> **Prayer:** Heavenly Father, as the reader begins this 40-day transformation journey, I pray that you embrace the identity God has given you. May you find the courage to step away from the

expectations of others and walk confidently in the truth of who you are in Christ.

I ask that your heart be filled with the assurance that you are not defined by the standards of this world but by His everlasting love. Just as Muhammad Ali declared his freedom to be who he was meant to be, may you also find the strength to live authentically, true to the person God has created you to be.

Task: Write down the specific change you want to make. Be as detailed as possible about what you want to achieve.

BOOK TITLE

Notes

Day 2: Understand Your Why

Ali's Quote:
"Service to others is the rent you pay for your room here on earth."

Scripture: *"Just as the Son of Man did not come to be served, but to serve, and to give His life as a ransom for many."* - Matthew 20:28

Prayer: Heavenly Father, thank You for the gift of life and the opportunities You have given the reader to serve others. Help them to understand their purpose in Your kingdom and to live a life of service, just as Jesus did. Let their actions reflect Your love and grace, and may they find joy in giving of themselves to others. In Jesus' name, Amen.

Understand Your Why

The early morning sunlight peeked through my curtains, casting a gentle light across the room. I sat at the edge of my bed, my mind racing with thoughts of the day ahead. Yesterday, I took the first step in my 40-day journey—deciding that I needed to change. But today, I knew I had to go deeper. I needed to understand my "why."

With a deep breath, I reached for my journal, the pages already filled with thoughts, prayers, and hopes for the future. As I opened a fresh page, I found myself staring at the blank space, unsure of where to start. Why am I doing this? What is it that drives me to make this change? The answers didn't come easily, and that troubled me.

I closed my eyes and let my mind wander back to my childhood. I could see my uncle, Muhammad Ali, not just as the world saw him—a champion in the ring—but as I knew him. He was a man who lived for something greater than himself. I remembered how he often spoke about the importance of service, about how life wasn't just about being the greatest boxer but about making a difference in the lives of others. "Service to others is the rent you pay for your room here on earth," he'd say. Those words echoed in my mind, and suddenly, I felt a connection to something more profound.

It hit me that my "why" isn't just about shedding pounds or getting fit. It's about becoming the best version of myself to help others and inspire and lift them up, just like my uncle did. But I know that to do that, I first must lift myself up. I need to be strong, not just in my body but also in my mind and spirit.

The scripture I read this morning, Matthew 20:28—"Just as the Son of Man did not come to be served, but to serve, and to give His life as a ransom for many"—spoke directly to my heart. My journey isn't just about me. It's about preparing myself to serve others and to fulfill the purpose God has laid out for me. My uncle lived by that principle, and now I understand that this journey is about more than just my own transformation. It's about honoring his legacy and creating one of my own.

I picked up my pen and began to write in my journal. "I'm doing this because I want to be strong for those who can't be. I'm doing this to honor my uncle's legacy and to create one of my own. I'm doing this to serve, love, and inspire."

As I wrote, a sense of peace washed over me. I understood my "why" brought clarity and focus I hadn't felt before. I knew there would be tough days ahead, but with a clear "why," I could face them with courage and determination.

Closing my journal, I stood up, feeling a newfound resolve. Today was about understanding—digging deep into the reasons behind my journey. And with that understanding, I knew I could tackle whatever lay ahead. This journey was no longer just about me; it was about something much bigger. It was about becoming the man God has called me to be.

I walked out of my room, ready to face the challenges of the day. I had a prayer in my heart and my "why" firmly in mind. Each step I took would bring me closer to fulfilling my purpose.

Prophetic Word on Understanding Your Why

The Lord is speaking to you today about the importance of knowing the "why" behind your actions. He is saying, "I have placed a purpose within you, a deep calling that goes beyond the surface of what you do. It is rooted in love, service, and the heart of My will for your life."

God encourages you to reflect on your motivations, dig deep, and discover the true reasons behind the changes you are pursuing. "When you understand your 'why,' you align yourself with My purpose," says the Lord. "This clarity will give you the strength to persevere, even when the journey is tough."

The Lord also reminds you that your purpose is not just about personal fulfillment but about serving others. "Just as My Son came not to be served, but to serve," says the Lord, "so too have I called you to serve those around you. You will find true meaning in serving, and your life will reflect My love to the world."

As you reflect on your motivations, the Lord fills you with a renewed sense of purpose. "Let your actions be rooted in love and service," he says. "This path leads to true fulfillment and lasting impact."

Take this time to understand your "why" and allow it to guide you in every decision. The Lord is with you, empowering you to live a life that is purposeful, meaningful, and aligned with His divine plan.

> **Prayer:** Heavenly Father, help the reader to understand their purpose and the deeper reasons for their journey. May their actions be rooted in love and service to others. Amen.

Task: Take time today to reflect on how you can serve others. Write down one way you will use your gifts to help someone in need this week, whether through a kind word, a helping hand, or simply being present for someone who needs support.

BOOK TITLE

Notes

Day 3: Set Clear, Achievable Goals

Ali's Quote: *"It isn't the mountains ahead to climb that wear you out; it's the pebble in your shoe."*

Scripture: *"For which of you, intending to build a tower, does not sit down first and count the cost, whether he has enough to finish it."* - Luke 14:28

Prayer: Heavenly Father, guide the reader as they set their goals. Help them to plan wisely, removing the small obstacles that hinder their progress. Amen.

Embracing Change: My Commitment

We often talk about change, but when it comes time to embrace it, that's where the real challenge begins. For me, the decision to embrace change didn't happen overnight. It was a gradual realization brought on by years of feeling stuck in a cycle that no longer served me. I had gotten comfortable with the status quo, even though deep down, I knew I was capable of more.

The turning point came on a quiet evening when I reflected on where I was in life. I looked around at the cluttered room, the pile of unfinished projects, and the goals I had once been so passionate about but had since abandoned. It was like a mirror reflecting at me the state of my inner world—scattered, unfocused, and weighed down by a sense of inertia.

That night, I decided. I realized that if I didn't commit to change, I would continue to drift, missing out on the opportunities and growth that awaited me. I thought about the kind of life I wanted to lead—the person I wanted to become. I knew it wouldn't be easy, but I was determined to break free from the habits and mindsets holding me back.

The following morning, I woke up with a sense of purpose I hadn't felt in a long time. I took out a notebook and began writing down the changes I needed to make. They weren't grandiose or overwhelming; they were small, manageable steps I could take each day. I committed to waking up earlier, exercising, and decluttering my space physically and mentally. But more importantly, I committed to believing in myself and the possibility of change.

Each day since then has been a practice in embracing change. There have been setbacks, moments where I've doubted myself, and times when I've wanted to give up. But each time, I remind myself of why I started. Change isn't about perfection; it's about progress. It's about showing up every day, even when it's hard, and believing the effort will pay off.

In embracing change, I've discovered a strength within myself that I didn't know was there. I've learned that I am capable of more than I ever imagined and that my only limits are the ones I place on myself. This journey isn't over—change is a continuous process—but I'm committed to seeing it through. I'm committed to becoming the best version of myself, one step at a time.

Training and Setting Goals: The Mission

The decision to follow in my uncle's footsteps was not one I made lightly. Growing up, I was always aware of Muhammad Ali's legacy—the world's greatest boxer, a man of immense strength, both physically and spiritually. But it was not until I was faced with my own challenges—being 110 pounds overweight, struggling with addiction, and feeling lost in life—that I utterly understood what it meant to fight, not just in the ring but in life.

When I decided to take on the mission of transforming my life, I knew that training would be at the heart of it. But this was not about losing weight or getting fit. It was about setting goals aligned with the man I wanted to become—strong, disciplined, and focused.

The first step was acknowledging where I was. I stood in front of the mirror, taking in the reflection staring back at me. I saw the weight I had gained, the toll that unhealthy habits had taken on my body, and the fatigue that clouded my mind. But I also saw potential. I saw a man who was ready to fight for his future.

I began by setting small, achievable goals. My first goal was establishing a routine—something I could stick to daily. I woke up earlier, dedicating time to exercise and prayer before the day began. It wasn't easy at first; my body protested the sudden changes, and there were mornings when the last thing I wanted to do was get out of bed. But I pushed through, reminding myself of why I was doing this.

As I trained, I could hear my uncle's voice in my head telling me to keep going, push harder, and believe in myself. I started running, something I had not done in years. At first, I could barely make it a few blocks without feeling winded, but I went a little further each day. I also began strength training, focusing on building the muscle and endurance I knew I would need, not just for my physical transformation but for the battles I would face mentally and spiritually.

Setting goals was crucial. I did not just set one big goal to lose weight; I broke it down into smaller milestones. The first was to lose ten pounds. Then, it was to run a mile without stopping. Each goal I achieved fueled my determination to keep going.

But more than the physical training, I worked on my mindset. I knew that if I wanted to succeed, I had to change the way I thought about myself and my abilities. I started reading more, studying the greats—athletes, leaders, and thinkers—who had achieved greatness not just through talent but through sheer will and discipline.

Every day, I reminded myself of my mission. This was not just about me but about the people I could inspire and the lives I could touch. I wanted to show others that it's never too late to change and that you can always get back up, no matter how far you've fallen.

As I continue my training, I'm more focused than ever. My goals are clear, my routine is set, and my mind is stronger. There are still days when it's tough when the weight of the mission feels heavy. But I keep going, knowing that every step I take, every goal I reach, brings me closer to the man I was meant to be—a man who fights not just for himself but for a greater purpose.

Prophetic Word on Setting Goals

The Lord is speaking to you today about the importance of setting clear and achievable goals. He says, "I have placed dreams and desires in your heart for a reason, but I am also a God of order and wisdom. Just as I have crafted the universe with precision, I also desire for you to approach your goals with intentionality and clarity."

God is encouraging you to take the time to plan and to count the cost of what it will take to achieve your goals. "Do not rush into things," says the Lord, "but sit down and consider what is needed. When you plan with My wisdom, you will find that even the mountains ahead of you can be scaled without fear."

The Lord also wants you to be aware of the "pebbles" in your path—the small obstacles that can wear you out if left unchecked. "Bring these before Me," He says, "and I will help you to remove them. Do not let these small things hinder the great work I have called you to accomplish."

As you set your goals, the Lord reminds you that He is with you in every step. "Commit your plans to Me," He says, "and I will establish them. I will give you the strength, the wisdom, and the perseverance you need to see them through to completion."

Know that as you take these steps to set clear goals, you are aligning yourself with God's purpose for your life. He is guiding you, removing obstacles, and equipping you for success. Trust in His timing, and move forward confidently, knowing He is leading you every step of the way.

> **Prayer:** Heavenly Father may the reader lean on Your wisdom and be fearless as the mountains seem too high to climb.

Task: Break down your overall goal into smaller, actionable steps. Write these steps down in a planner or journal.

BOOK TITLE

Notes

Day 4: Visualize Success

Ali's Quote: *"What you're thinking is what you're becoming."*

Scripture: *"Finally, brethren, whatever things are true, whatever things are noble, whatever things are just, whatever things are pure, whatever things are lovely, whatever things are of good report, if there is any virtue and if there is anything praiseworthy—meditate on these things."* - Philippians 4:8

Prayer: Heavenly Father, may the reader's thoughts be aligned with Your truth, leading them to become who You created them to be. Amen.

Defending My Cruiserweight Title: The Fight Within

The gym was my sanctuary—a place where I could focus, where the world outside faded away, leaving only the sound of my breath, the rhythm of my movements, and the echo of my uncle's words in my mind. Posters of legendary fighters lined the walls, their eyes fierce with determination, their bodies carved from years of relentless training. I looked at them every day, drawing strength from their legacy, knowing that I was part of that lineage and had a title to defend.

As I began my warm-up, I reached for the jump rope hanging on the wall. The worn handles felt familiar in my hands, and as I started to skip, the rope whistled through the air in a steady, rhythmic pattern. Each jump was a heartbeat, a reminder of why I was here. My mind started to wander, but it wasn't a distraction—no, this was part of the process. I wasn't just jumping rope; I was stepping into the ring in my imagination, facing the challenger who wanted to take what I had fought so hard to earn.

I could see him in my mind's eye—a towering figure, muscles taut, his eyes locked on mine with a look of fierce determination. He was relentless, a fighter with everything to prove. I imagined the way he would move, his footwork sharp, his punches fast and precise. I knew he would come at me with everything he had, trying to find a weakness and exploit any moment of hesitation.

But there would be no hesitation. I increased the speed of my jumps, and the rope blurred beneath my feet. My breathing quickened, but I kept my form tight, my focus unshakable. Yes, I was preparing my body, but more importantly, I was preparing my mind. In the ring, it's not just about who hits harder—it's about who can think faster, adapt, and outlast the other.

As I moved to the speed bag, I could feel the sweat beginning to bead on my forehead. The sound of the bag as it rebounded against the platform was like music—a steady, rhythmic beat that matched the tempo of my heart. I imagined the challenger's fast, brutal punches designed to take me down. But I was faster. Each tap of the speed bag was a counterpunch, and each beat was a reminder that I could outpace him and anticipate his every move.

In my mind, the fight was unfolding with vivid detail. I saw us circling each other in the ring, the crowd's roar a distant hum, drowned out by the pounding of my heart and the sound of leather meeting flesh. I could feel the tension in the air, the electric charge that only a championship fight can bring. My challenger would be hungry—hungry for the title, hungry for victory. But I was hungrier.

I imagined the moment he would try to break through my defense, throwing a flurry of punches meant to overwhelm me. But I was ready. My footwork was light, my guard up. I could see his movements before he made them, as if the fight was choreographed just for me. A jab, a cross, a hook—I countered each one in my mind, the speed bag responding to my every thought, my hands a blur of motion.

As I worked the bag, the sweat dripping down my face, I could feel the fight intensifying in my mind. My challenger was relentless, but so was I. I countered every punch he threw with precision and power. I imagined the look in his eyes when he realized that no matter how hard he fought, I wasn't going to give up. I wasn't going to back down.

The final round played out in my head as I pushed myself harder, the speed bag moving faster than ever. The bell rang in my imagination, signaling the end of the fight. I could see the exhaustion in my challenger's eyes, his body bruised and battered. But I stood tall, my body aching but still strong, still ready to fight.

As I finished my workout, the images in my mind began to fade, replaced by the sounds of the gym—weights clanging, the grunts of other fighters training, the hum of the air conditioning. But the feeling remained—the confidence that came from knowing I was ready, that I had prepared for every possibility, that I was mentally and physically strong enough to defend my title.

This fight wasn't just about retaining a belt; it was about proving to myself that I could rise to the occasion and overcome any challenge. Every drop of sweat, every moment of pain, every hour spent training was an investment in that belief. And when the day came to step into the ring, I would be ready—not just because of the work I had put in, but because of the fighter I had become in the process.

The title was mine, and I was ready to defend it.

Prophetic Word on Visualizing Success

The Lord is calling you to align your thoughts with His truth, for what you focus on has the power to shape your destiny. I hear the Lord saying, "As you meditate on what is true, noble, and praiseworthy, you are not just shaping your thoughts but your future. I have placed within you the ability to visualize success, to see beyond the present into the fulfillment of the dreams I have given you."

God is encouraging you to take time each day to visualize the success He has in store for you. "Picture it," says the Lord, "as vividly as you can. See yourself walking in the fullness of My plans, achieving the goals that align with My purpose for your life. As you do this, you are stepping into the reality of My promises."

The Lord is also reminding you that your thoughts have the power to transform your life. "What you think, you become," he says. "Let My Spirit guide your thoughts, and you will find that they lead you into a place of victory and abundance."

As you visualize success, remember that you are not doing this alone. The Lord is with you, guiding your thoughts, inspiring your imagination, and strengthening your resolve. "Meditate on My word, and let it fill your mind with My truth," He says. "As you do this, you will find that your thoughts begin to align with My plans, and you will become the person I created you to be."

Take this time to see yourself as God sees you—victorious, empowered, and full of purpose. Let this vision of success propel you forward, knowing that with God, all things are possible.

> **Prayer:** Heavenly Father, thank You for the power of our thoughts and the vision You have placed within us. As we visualize success, we ask that You guide our minds to dwell on what is true, noble, and praiseworthy. Help us to see ourselves through Your eyes, becoming who You have created us to be. Strengthen our faith to believe that what we envision in alignment with Your will can be achieved. Let our thoughts and actions move us closer to the purpose You have set before us. In Jesus' name, Amen.

Task: Spend 5-10 minutes each morning visualizing yourself achieving your goal. Picture it as vividly as possible.

Notes

Day 5: Create a Plan

Ali's Quote: *"The fight is won or lost far away from witnesses—behind the lines, in the gym, and out there on the road, long before I dance under those lights."*

Scripture: *"Commit your works to the Lord, and your thoughts will be established."* - Proverbs 16:3

Prayer: Heavenly Father, bless the reader's plans and efforts. May they diligently prepare, knowing that You guide their steps. Amen.

Creating a Plan – The Journey

When I decided to step into the ring and pursue boxing seriously, I knew having a vision was essential. But a vision without a plan is just a dream. If I wanted to honor my uncle's legacy and carve out my own path, I needed more than just desire—I needed a concrete plan that would guide me through the grueling months of preparation leading up to my next fight.

It was one of those mornings in the gym when the sweat started pouring before I even threw my first punch. Coach Moses was waiting for me, his eyes scanning the room, making mental notes of what needed to be done. "Today, we're going to map out your fight plan," he said, his tone leaving no room for anything less than total commitment. The day wasn't just about training; it was about strategy, about knowing exactly what needed to be done and when.

We started by breaking down the fight. Moses talked me through the different scenarios I might face in the ring. "What if your opponent tries to rush you in the first round? What if he plays defense and waits for you to make a mistake?" He threw questions at me like jabs, each forcing me to think, anticipate, and prepare.

As we worked through the plan, it became clear that this wasn't just about physical conditioning. It was about mental preparation, about being ready for anything that could happen in the ring. I wrote everything down in my training journal—the drills I needed to focus on, the combinations I had to perfect, the endurance work that would ensure I could go the distance. Each day had a purpose, and each session had a goal.

Proverbs 16:3 says, "Commit your works to the Lord, and your thoughts will be established." That verse became a cornerstone of my plan. I wasn't just committing to the work; I was dedicating it to a higher purpose, trusting that God would guide my steps if I put in the effort. My plan wasn't just about winning a fight but also aligning my actions with my faith and vision.

As I punched the heavy bag that day, I wasn't just releasing energy but executing a plan; each strike was calculated, and each movement was deliberate. I could feel the difference that having a plan made. The doubts that usually lingered in the back of my mind started to fade, replaced by a growing confidence. I knew where I was going and how I was going to get there.

Those of you reading this understand that creating a plan is crucial. It's easy to get overwhelmed by the big picture, to feel like the mountain is too high to climb. But when you break it down into steps and create a roadmap, it becomes manageable. Whether your goal is to get in shape, start a new career, or overcome a personal challenge, you need a plan. Write it down. Make it specific. And then commit to it with everything you've got.

Remember, champions aren't just made in the gym—they're made in the mind. The fight is won or lost long before you step into the ring, in the daily decisions you make, in the plan you follow with discipline and determination. So, take the time to create your plan, and trust that as you commit to it, you'll find the strength and the guidance to see it through.

Prophetic Word:

The Lord says, "I have placed a vision within you, and now is the time to bring it to life with strategy and focus. Do not fear the steps ahead, for I am guiding you. I will open doors and provide the necessary resources as you commit your plans to Me. Every step you take in preparation is a step of faith, and I will bless your diligence. What may seem hidden now will be revealed in due time, and your work behind the scenes will set the stage for a victory far greater than you can imagine. Trust that I am with you, shaping and aligning every detail for My glory and your success."

> **Prayer:** Heavenly Father, thank You for the vision and purpose You have placed in our hearts. As we commit our plans and efforts to You, we trust that You will guide our steps and align our actions with Your will. Strengthen us in our preparation and give us the wisdom to navigate any challenges that may come our way. We place our confidence in You, knowing You are the source of all success. May every detail of our plan be blessed and directed by Your hand. In Jesus' name, Amen.

Task: Develop a detailed plan for how you will achieve your goals. Include timelines, resources, and potential obstacles.

BOOK TITLE

Notes

Day 6: Build a Support System

Ali's Quote: *"Friendship... is not something you learn in school. But if you haven't learned the meaning of friendship, you really haven't learned anything."*

Scripture: *"Two are better than one, because they have a good return for their labor: If either of them falls down, one can help the other up."* - Ecclesiastes 4:9-10

Prayer: Heavenly Father, surround the reader with supportive and encouraging people. May their relationships be strong and rooted in Your love. Amen.

Building a Support System – Ibn's Journey

As much as boxing is a solitary endeavor, one where you're alone in the ring facing your opponent, I've learned that you can't get there alone. Behind every fighter, there's a team—a group of people who push, guide, and believe in you even when you're too exhausted to believe in yourself. For me, that team has always included my father. While Coach Moses was the one who pushed me to my physical limits, it was my father who was my true confidant, my guiding light through the mental and emotional battles.

My father wasn't just someone who shared in my victories; he was ringside in my mind during every fight, even when he wasn't physically there. We had this routine of talking after my training sessions. I'd call him, no matter how late, and we'd have these incredible conversations. He'd share stories about my uncle, Muhammad Ali, about the fights he witnessed up close, the moments of strategy, and the words exchanged in the corner between rounds.

I remember one conversation vividly. It was after a grueling day of training that I felt like I had nothing left to give. My muscles were screaming, my mind was clouded with fatigue, and doubt had started to creep in. I called my father, hoping for some encouragement, and as always, he picked up after the first ring.

"How'd it go today, son?" he asked, his voice steady and warm.

"It was tough, Dad," I admitted. "Coach Moses really pushed me. I'm exhausted, and honestly, I'm not sure how much more I can take."

There was a pause on the other end, and I could hear him thinking. Then, he started talking, not about me, but about a fight my uncle had years ago. "You know, I was ringside for your uncle's fight against Joe Frazier, the first one. The whole world was watching. People were calling it the

'Fight of the Century.' But what they didn't see, what they couldn't know, was the fight that was going on in your uncle's mind. Between rounds, when he'd come back to the corner, there were moments when he looked so tired and beaten, but he'd always listen to the corner, always take in the advice, and go back out there ready to fight again."

As he spoke, I could almost see it—my uncle sitting in the corner, his body bruised, sweat dripping down his face, but his eyes focused and determined. My father continued, "Your uncle wasn't just fighting Frazier in that ring. He was fighting to prove something to himself, to the world. And every time he returned to the corner, he drew strength from us, from the people who believed in him. That's what I'm here for, Ibn. I'm in your corner, too, every step of the way."

Those words hit me like a jolt of energy. I realized then that my father wasn't just telling me a story; he reminded me that I wasn't alone. Just like my uncle had his corner, I had mine. I had people who believed in me and invested in my success, not just in the ring but in life.

It's easy to think that strength comes from within, and while that's true, I've learned that the people around you help you find that strength when you're running low. My father, with his wisdom and his stories, has always been a source of strength for me. He's the voice that cuts through the noise, the one who helps me see the bigger picture when I'm too focused on the pain of the moment.

For those of you reading this, I can't stress enough the importance of building a support system. Whether it's a parent, a friend, or a mentor, find someone who believes in you, someone who will be in your corner no matter what. Share your goals with them, ask for their encouragement, and lean on them when the going gets tough. Because when you're in the middle of a fight—whether in the ring or in life—those people will help you dig deep and find the champion within.

Prophetic Word on Building a Support System

The Lord is highlighting the importance of relationships in your life right now. He says, "I have placed people around you for a reason. You are not meant to walk this journey alone. Just as I designed the body to have many parts, so have I designed your life to be enriched by your connections with others." God is encouraging you to reach out and build and strengthen the support system around you. "Two are better than one," says the Lord, "because together you can accomplish more, and when one stumbles, the other can lift them up." It is a time to be intentional about the relationships in your life, to invest in those who encourage you, uplift you, and walk alongside you in your journey.

The Lord also reminds you that these relationships are a gift from Him, rooted in His love. "As you build your support system," He says, "let it be grounded in My love, which binds everything together in perfect harmony. Let your friendships and connections reflect My heart for you—a heart that desires your growth, joy, and success."

Do not hesitate to share your goals and dreams with those you trust. God is saying, "I have placed people in your life who will champion your cause, pray for you, and stand with you through thick and thin. Lean on them, and allow them to lean on you, for this is how I have designed you to thrive."

As you build and nurture these relationships, you will find that your journey becomes lighter, your steps more confident, and your heart fuller of hope. Remember, you are not alone—God is with you and has surrounded you with others to walk this path with you.

> **Prayer:** Heavenly Father, as we take this time to rest and reflect, we thank You for the strength and guidance You've given us so far. We acknowledge that true rest comes from You and ask that You renew our minds and spirits for the journey ahead. Please help us find peace in our progress and grant us the perseverance to keep moving forward when we rise again. May we continue to walk in Your purpose with

renewed energy and focus. In Jesus' name, Amen.

Task: Contact a friend or family member who can support you in your journey. Share your goals with them and ask for their encouragement.

Notes

Day 7: Rest and Reflect

Ali's Quote: *"Rest but never quit. Even the sun has a sinking spell each evening. But it always rises the next morning."*

Scripture: *"Come to me, all you who are weary and burdened, and I will give you rest."* – Matthew 11:28

Prayer: Heavenly Father, grant the reader rest and rejuvenation. Help them to reflect on their progress and renew their strength for the journey ahead. Amen.

A Lesson on Rest

Sometimes, the most significant lessons in life come from unexpected moments when the universe forces you to pause, even when you think you can't afford to. I experienced one of those moments not too long ago while preparing for a crucial fight.

I was deep into my training camp, working harder than ever to ensure I was ready for the challenge ahead. Every day was a grind—hours spent in the gym, pushing my body to the brink, honing my skills, and sharpening my mind. My coach, Moses, had planned a particularly intense session that day. We were going to focus on endurance, with back-to-back rounds on the heavy bag, mitt work, and some serious conditioning drills. I was mentally prepared for a brutal day.

But as I was wrapping my hands and getting ready to hit the gym, the sky outside began to darken. The rain started pouring down within minutes, harder than I'd seen in a long time. It wasn't just a regular storm; it was a full-blown deluge, the kind that turns streets into rivers and sends people scrambling for cover. I didn't think much of it at first. Rain or shine, training had to go on. But as I stepped into the gym, I realized this storm was different.

The power flickered once, then again, before going out completely. The hum of the lights, the whir of the fans, the sound of the music in the background—all of it ceased, leaving the gym in an eerie silence, broken only by the sound of the rain pounding on the roof. The gym plunged into darkness, with only the occasional flash of lightning illuminating the space.

Coach Moses came out from the office, his face a mixture of frustration and resignation. "Looks like we're out of business for a while, champ," he said, shaking his head. "No power, no lights, no way to train in here today."

I could see the disappointment on the faces of the other fighters as they began to pack up, but I wasn't ready to quit. I had too much on the line, too much riding on this fight. "What do we do now?" I asked Moses, hoping he had a solution.

He thought for a moment, then smiled, a glint of challenge in his eyes. "We adapt, Ibn. The gym's not the only place to train. Let's see what you're made of outside."

We stepped out into the storm, the rain instantly soaking us to the bone. The streets were nearly empty, the kind of scene you'd expect in a disaster movie, but this was no disaster; it was an opportunity. The wet pavement, the wind howling through the trees, the cold sting of the rain on my skin—it all became part of the training.

Coach Moses started me off with some basic footwork drills, but the slippery ground added a whole new level of difficulty. Every step had to be calculated and every movement deliberate. I had to adjust my balance constantly, learning to stay grounded even as the world around me was anything but stable.

Next came shadowboxing, the wind providing natural resistance that made each punch harder, each movement more taxing. The rain was relentless, but so was I. Every drop that hit my face felt like a reminder that life doesn't always go according to plan. But champions aren't made when everything's going smoothly. Champions are made when they adapt and find a way to keep moving forward, no matter the circumstances.

As the rain continued to pour, Coach Moses and I found shelter under a large tree in the park. The workout was intense, but there was something almost serene about it. The storm was raging, but within me, was a sense of calm, of focus. I realized that this unexpected training day was teaching me something far more valuable than any session in the gym ever could.

When the rain finally began to let up and the storm clouds started to break apart, Moses called it a day. "That was good work, Ibn. Real good. But remember, even champions need rest."

We walked back to the gym, now just a dark building with no power, and I knew he was right. The day hadn't gone as planned, but it had given me exactly what I needed—a reminder that rest is as crucial as training and that sometimes, stepping back and reflecting is the best way to move forward.

I took the rest of the day to rest and reflect, just as the storm had forced me to do. I thought about the progress I had made that week, not just physically but mentally and emotionally. I realized that every setback and challenge was a part of the journey, shaping me into the fighter I was meant to be.

For those of you reading this, remember that rest isn't a sign of weakness. It's a necessary part of growth. Take the time to reflect on your progress to acknowledge how far you've come. And know that even when the lights go out, when the storm hits, there's always a way forward. Sometimes, it's in the rest that you find the strength to rise again.

Prophetic Word on Rest and Reflection

The Lord is inviting you into a place of rest today, reminding you that rest is not a sign of weakness but a source of strength. I hear the Lord saying, "Come to Me, all who are weary, and I will give you rest. It is time to lay down your burdens and allow Me to renew your strength for the journey ahead."

God wants you to know that in these moments of rest and reflection, He often does His deepest work within you. "As you rest, I am working," says the Lord. "I am renewing your mind, refreshing your spirit, and restoring your soul. Do not be afraid to pause, for it is in the quiet that you will hear My voice most clearly."

The Lord is also encouraging you to take time to reflect on the progress you have made. "Look back and see how far you have come," He says. "I have been with you every step of the way, guiding you, providing for you, and strengthening you. Let this reflection fill your heart with gratitude and give you the courage to continue moving forward."

As you rest today, the Lord is pouring His peace upon you. He reminds you that rest is not the end of your journey but a necessary pause that prepares you for the next steps. "Take this time to be still and know that I am God," He says. "I am your source of strength, and I will never leave you nor forsake you."

Allow yourself to rest in His presence, knowing He is with you, guiding you, and preparing you for what lies ahead.

> **Prayer:** Heavenly Father, thank You for the gift of rest and reflection. As we pause from our efforts today, we ask that You renew our minds, bodies, and spirits. Help us see our progress, no matter how small, and give us the strength and courage to continue the journey ahead. May this time of rest fill us with Your peace and prepare us for the next steps with a refreshed sense of purpose. We trust in Your guidance and provision for the days to come. In Jesus' name, Amen.

Task: Take a break from actively working on your goal. Spend some time reflecting on the progress you've made this week.

Notes

Week 2: Building Momentum

Day 8: Start Small

Ali's Quote: *"He who is not courageous enough to take risks will accomplish nothing in life."*

Scripture: *"Have I not commanded you? Be strong and courageous. Do not be afraid; do not be discouraged, for the Lord your God will be with you wherever you go."* - Joshua 1:9

Prayer: Heavenly Father, give the reader the courage to take the first steps, no matter how small. May they trust in Your presence as they move forward. Amen.

Start Small – Ibn's Journey

The road to greatness isn't paved overnight; it's built brick by brick, small step by small step. I've always believed that, but the truth of it hit me hard when I first started my boxing career. Unlike most fighters, I didn't have the luxury of an amateur record filled with wins and losses to learn from. My path was different—much like the story in the movie "Creed," where a name opened doors that would usually have taken years of blood, sweat, and tears to unlock. The name Ali opened those doors for me, and suddenly, I found myself standing in a place where there was no room for small beginnings—at least, that's what it seemed like.

But that wasn't entirely true. Even with a name like mine, the reality is that every journey begins with a single step, and those steps are often small, even if they don't appear that way to others. I learned early on that courage isn't about making giant leaps; it's about taking that first step, no matter how small, and trusting that each one will lead to something greater.

I remember the first time I walked into the gym where I'd begin my professional career. The air was thick with the smell of sweat and leather, and the sounds of fists meeting bags and trainers shouting instructions filled the space. I was nervous—no, I was terrified. Everyone in that gym knew who I was, and they expected me to live up to the name. But inside, I felt like a beginner, just another guy trying to figure it all out.

My first day of training wasn't anything spectacular; it was humbling, to say the least. Coach Moses didn't start me off with the heavy bag or the sparring ring. No, he handed me a jump rope and told me to start skipping. It seemed almost ridiculous, almost beneath me. Jumping rope? With everything that was expected of me, how could that be the first step?

But I did it. I grabbed that rope and started to skip. At first, I was clumsy, tripping over my own feet, the rope slapping against my shins, the sound of it missing rhythmically against the gym floor. But as I kept at it, something started to change. My coordination improved, my feet moved faster, and I started to feel the rhythm. What began as a simple, almost trivial task became the foundation of my training. I didn't know it then, but every moment spent jumping rope prepared me for the ring in ways I couldn't have imagined.

Each small step built on the one before it. The jump rope led to shadowboxing, which led to hitting the speed bag, which led to footwork drills. I didn't see the results immediately, but that didn't matter. What mattered was that I kept moving forward, trusting that the process would lead me where I needed to go.

It's easy to get caught up in the idea that progress should be immediate and that results should come quickly, especially when there's pressure to live up to a legacy. But real progress is often slow and steady. It's in the small beginnings, the daily grind, the simple, repetitive tasks that might seem insignificant but are laying the groundwork for something much bigger.

For those of you reading this, I want you to know that starting small is okay. Don't be discouraged if you don't see results right away. The most important thing is to take that first step, no matter how small it may seem, and to keep moving forward. Those small actions will build momentum over time, whether it's making a phone call, starting a new habit, or just showing up.

Courage isn't just about the big moments; it's about having the strength to take small steps in the face of uncertainty. So today, take that step. Don't worry about the result just yet. Focus on what you can do right now, in this moment, and trust that every step you take will bring you closer to your goal.

Remember, "He who is not courageous enough to take risks will accomplish nothing in life." Be strong and courageous, knowing God is with you wherever you go. Each small step is a victory, a brick laid on the path to your dreams. Keep moving forward; soon, you'll look back and realize just how far you've come.

Prophetic Word on Starting Small

The Lord is encouraging you today to take that first step, no matter how small it may seem. I hear the Lord saying, "Do not despise the day of small beginnings, for I am with you in every step you take. The journey of a thousand miles begins with a single step, and it is in these first steps that your faith is tested and strengthened."

God is calling you to be courageous, not in the absence of fear, but in the midst of it. "I am your strength and your shield," says the Lord, "and as you move forward, you will find that My presence goes before you, making a way where there seems to be no way."

The Lord wants you to know that even the smallest actions, when done in faith, can profoundly impact your life and the lives of those around you. "Trust in My timing and My plan," says the Lord. "As you take these small steps, I will open doors, provide opportunities, and fulfill the dreams I have placed in your heart."

Do not be discouraged by the size of your beginnings, for God is the one who multiplies the seed that is sown. He says, "Plant your seed in faith, take that step, and watch as I bring the increase. I am with you wherever you go, and I will never leave you nor forsake you."

Take courage today and move forward, knowing that the Lord your God is with you every step of the way.

>**Prayer:** Heavenly Father, thank You for the courage You have instilled in us to take the first steps toward our goals. As we embrace the

small beginnings, we trust in Your guidance and presence with us every step of the way. Strengthen our resolve to keep moving forward, even when the path seems uncertain. Help us to remember that no step is too small when done in faith. May we walk boldly and confidently, knowing that You are with us wherever we go. In Jesus' name, Amen.

Task: Take a small step today toward your goal. It could be as simple as making a phone call, researching, or starting a new habit.

Notes

Day 9: Establish Routines

Ali's Quote: *"If they can make penicillin out of moldy bread, they can sure make something out of you."*

Scripture: *"But everything should be done in a fitting and orderly way."* - 1 Corinthians 14:40:

Prayer: Heavenly Father, help the reader establish routines that bring order and peace to their life. May their daily habits reflect Your will. Amen.

Establish Routines – My Journey

I'm Ibn Ali, Muhammad Ali's nephew. Growing up with the legacy of a legend in my family meant that expectations were always high. Early in life, I knew I had to carve out my own path to prove to myself and the world that I wasn't just riding on the coattails of my uncle's greatness. My journey has been one of discipline, rigorous training, and, most importantly, establishing routines that have become the backbone of my success.

One of the most pivotal moments in my life came when I was preparing for a major championship fight. My opponent was a powerhouse known for his raw strength and relentless aggression. The media was buzzing with doubts about whether I could handle him. But I knew this fight was about more than just claiming a title; it was about proving that the routines I had built over the years would carry me through any challenge.

My training regimen was intense but also structured—every part of my day had its purpose. I woke up at dawn each morning, and my routine started with running miles through the city streets. Each step was more than just a physical exercise; it was meditation, a way to align my mind and spirit with my goals. Like the deer mentioned in Psalm 18:33-34, my feet were swift and sure, guided by faith. My coach, Moses, who had been with me since the beginning, always reminded me of the importance of order and discipline. "If they can make penicillin out of moldy bread, they can sure make something out of you," he'd say, urging me to see the potential in every moment, every routine.

In the gym, I trained with a purpose. My hands were trained for battle, and every punch was delivered with precision and intent. My strength didn't come overnight—it resulted from countless hours spent honing my skills, building my endurance, and trusting the process. My faith was my anchor, and I knew that God was with me, guiding me through every punch, every round.

But the real secret to my success was the routine I had established. Each day, I followed a strict schedule: early morning runs, mid-morning gym sessions, afternoon strategy meetings, and evening reflection and prayer. Everything was done in order, with discipline and consistency. My routine wasn't just about physical training; it was about mental and spiritual preparation as well. I set aside time daily to reflect, pray, and visualize my goals. This routine kept me focused and brought peace and order to the chaos of preparing for a fight.

When the night of the fight finally arrived, I was ready—not just because of the physical work I had put in, but because my routine had prepared me mentally and spiritually for the challenge ahead. As I stepped into the ring, I felt a calm confidence wash over me. I knew I had done everything in my power to prepare, and the rest was in God's hands.

The fight was brutal, just as I expected. My opponent came at me with everything he had, but I was ready. My movements were precise, my punches powerful. I could feel the years of training, the routines I had established, coming together in that moment. With each round, I grew stronger and more confident. My routine had built not just my body but my mind and spirit, giving me the strength to face whatever came my way.

In the final round, my opponent unleashed a desperate flurry of attacks, but I stood my ground. My routine had taught me resilience, patience, and the ability to adapt. With one final, decisive blow, I sent him to the mat. The referee's count seemed to last forever, but when it was over, victory was mine. The crowd erupted, but I stood there quietly, knowing that it wasn't just the fight I had won—it was the years of discipline and the power of routine that brought me to this moment.

For those of you reading this, remember that greatness isn't achieved overnight. It's the result of daily routines, consistent effort, and unwavering faith. Create a routine that supports your goals, no matter how small the steps may seem initially. Trust in the process, and know that with order and discipline, you can achieve anything.

Prophetic Word on Establishing Routines

The Lord is speaking to you today about the power of establishing routines that align with His purpose for your life. I hear the Lord saying, "I am a God of order, and I desire to bring order into every area of your life. As you establish routines, you create space for My peace and presence to dwell more fully in your daily activities."

God is encouraging you to start small, knowing that even the most minor changes can significantly impact over time. "Do not despise the day of small beginnings," says the Lord, "for these routines will build a foundation of discipline and faithfulness in your life."

The Lord says, "As you commit to these routines, I will multiply your efforts. What may seem like a simple habit will become a powerful tool in My hand to shape you, to prepare you, and to propel you toward the goals I have placed in your heart."

You are not doing this alone—God is with you, guiding each step and providing the strength you need to be consistent. As you establish routines that honor Him, your life will become more ordered, peaceful, and aligned with His will.
The Lord also reminds you that these routines are not just about productivity but about creating a rhythm of life that draws you closer to Him. Let your daily habits reflect His goodness and deepen your relationship with the One who loves you.

> **Prayer:** Heavenly Father, thank You for the wisdom and guidance You provide in helping us establish routines that bring order to our lives. As we create habits that support our goals, may they be aligned with Your will and bring peace to our hearts. Grant us the discipline to stay committed to the routines we set and let each small change draw us closer to fulfilling our purpose. We trust in Your guidance every step of the way. In Jesus' name, Amen.

Task: Create a daily routine that supports your goals. Start with one small change, like setting aside time for your new habit each day.

Notes

Day 10: Track Your Progress

Ali's Quote: *"It's not bragging if you can back it up."*

Scripture: *"Then the Lord replied: 'Write down the revelation and make it plain on tablets so that a herald may run with it."* - Habakkuk 2:2

Prayer: Heavenly Father, guide the reader in tracking their progress. May they see tangible evidence of Your work in their life, giving You all the glory. Amen.

A Conversation with My Father

I was young when my uncle Muhammad Ali was in his prime, too young to have witnessed any of his legendary fights live. But the stories I heard growing up were as vivid as if I had been ringside for every one of them. My father, Rahman, would often sit with me, sharing tales from those days, and it was in these moments I learned some of the most important lessons of my life.

One evening, as we sat together in the living room, I felt a bit overwhelmed with the training ahead of my next big fight. My father noticed the tension in my posture and the furrow in my brow. He had a way of knowing when something was weighing on me.

"What's on your mind, son?" he asked, his voice calm and steady, the voice that always brought me back to the center. "I'm just thinking about this next fight," I admitted. "There's so much pressure, and I'm not sure if I'm ready. It feels like there's so much to do, so much to prove."

My father leaned back in his chair, a knowing smile on his face. "You know, your uncle used to feel that way too, especially before a big fight. But he had a way of handling it that was... different."

I looked at him, curious. "What do you mean?"

"Well," he began, "you've probably heard how your uncle used to predict the round he'd knock out his opponent. People thought it was just him being brash and showing off. But it was more than that. Those predictions weren't just talk—they were based on something real, something he'd tracked and understood."

He could see he had my full attention now. "Your uncle didn't just wake up one day and decide, 'I'm going to knock this guy out in the fifth round.' No, he'd study his opponents meticulously. He'd watch tapes over and over, learning their patterns and their weaknesses. He knew them almost as well as he knew himself. But that wasn't all. He also knew his own strengths—how much power he had, how long he could keep up his pace, how his body responded in each round. He tracked everything."

"He'd watch his progress in training, noting how he felt after different exercises, how his punches landed during sparring. He knew exactly what he could do and when he could do it. So, when he called a round, it wasn't a guess—it was a calculated prediction based on facts, on the progress he'd tracked day in and day out."

I sat there, absorbing every word. "So it wasn't just about confidence," I said slowly. "It was about knowing he'd done the work and could back it up."

"Exactly," my father replied. "Your uncle always said, 'It's not bragging if you can back it up.' And he knew he could back it up because he had the evidence—the journals, the training logs, the mental notes—all tracking his progress. That's why he was so confident in those predictions. He wasn't just talking; he was telling the truth as he knew it."

I nodded, realizing that I needed to apply this to my training. "So, if I start tracking my progress—really paying attention to every detail—I'll be able to see where I stand, what I need to improve, and know when I'm ready."

"That's right," my father said with a smile. "Write it down, track it, and you'll see the difference. You'll know exactly where you are and what you're capable of. And when you step into that ring, you'll have that same confidence your uncle had because you'll know you've done the work."

That night, I started a new habit. I began keeping a detailed journal of my training, noting everything from how my body felt after a hard workout to my mental state during sparring sessions. I tracked my diet, sleep, and mindset—everything that could impact my performance. And slowly, I began to see the patterns, the areas where I was improving, and the places where I needed to push harder.

When fight night came, I knew I was ready. I had the proof in front of me; the records that showed my progress backed up my confidence. Like my uncle, I wasn't guessing I knew what I could do because I had tracked it every step of the way.

For those of you reading this, remember that tracking your progress isn't just about numbers or checkmarks on a list. It's about building confidence through preparation, knowing that you've done the work, and that you can back up every claim you make. So, start today. Track your progress, and you'll know you're ready when you face your own challenges.

Prophetic Word on Tracking Progress

The Lord is encouraging you today to diligently track your progress, not just in the tasks you accomplish but in the growth of your spirit and the fulfillment of the vision He has given you. I hear the Lord saying, "I have placed dreams and revelations within you, and I am calling you to steward them well. Writing down your progress is not just a practical step but an act of faith, acknowledging that I am at work in your life."

Just as Habakkuk was instructed to write down the vision, the Lord calls you to document the journey He leads you on. "Write it down," says the Lord, "so that you may see My hand in every detail and so that others may be encouraged by the testimony of what I am doing in your life."

This is not about boasting in your strength but giving glory to God for your progress. The Lord says, "As you track your progress, you will see My faithfulness in every step. You will be reminded of My promises and encouraged to press on toward the goal I have set before you."

Do not underestimate the power of recording your journey. Each entry is a stone of remembrance, a marker of God's grace and provision. As you reflect on what you have written, you will see how far He has brought you, and your faith will be strengthened for the future.

The Lord is with you, guiding each step, and as you commit your plans to Him, He will establish them. Keep going, keep writing, and let your progress be a testimony of His goodness in your life.

Prayer: Heavenly Father, thank You for our progress on this journey. As we track each step, help us see how far we've come and recognize Your hand in every success. Grant us the discipline to stay consistent, and let every achievement remind us of Your faithfulness in our lives. May we always give You the glory for the growth and transformation You are working within us. In Jesus' name, Amen.

Task: Begin tracking your daily progress. Use a journal, app, or planner to record your actions and results.

BOOK TITLE

Notes

Day 11: Overcome Mental Barriers

Ali's Quote: *"I hated every minute of training, but I said, 'Don't quit. Suffer now and live the rest of your life as a champion."*

Scripture: *"But he said to me, 'My grace is sufficient for you, for my power is made perfect in weakness.'"* - 2 Corinthians 12:9

Prayer: Heavenly Father, help the reader to overcome any mental barriers. Strengthen their weakness, and may Your grace sustain them through every challenge. Amen.

Overcoming Mental Barriers – My Journey

Growing up with the legacy of Muhammad Ali as my uncle, I was constantly surrounded by stories of his greatness, triumphs, and incredible willpower. However, one of the stories that always stuck with me was about how much he hated training. That might surprise some people because we often think of champions as loving every minute of the grind, but that wasn't the case for my uncle. He despised the pain, the exhaustion, the relentless effort it took to stay at the top. Yet, despite all that, he embraced it because he knew it was the only way to achieve greatness.

I remember my father telling me about the lead-up to one of Uncle Muhammad's most famous fights—The Rumble in the Jungle, when he faced George Foreman in 1974. Foreman was a beast in the ring, known for his devastating power and relentless aggression. He had knocked out his last eight opponents, most of them in the early rounds. The world was skeptical about whether my uncle could stand up to that kind of raw power, especially at that point in his career.

Training for that fight was grueling. My uncle knew he had to be in the best shape of his life, both physically and mentally. But the training sessions were brutal. He pushed his body to the limit every single day, running miles in the scorching heat, sparring endlessly, and enduring punishing rounds on the heavy bag. My father would often see him after those sessions, drenched in sweat, his muscles aching, his mind weary.

One evening, my uncle sat with my father and confided, "I hate every minute of this training. But I keep telling myself, 'Don't quit. Suffer now and live the rest of your life as a champion.'" Those words carried so much weight because they weren't just about that fight but about life. My uncle understood that success doesn't come easy; it comes from pushing through the pain, the discomfort, and the mental barriers that make you want to quit.

On the night of the fight, my uncle faced a seemingly unbeatable opponent. But he had a strategy, one that required immense mental fortitude. He used what would later be known as the "Rope-a-Dope" tactic, letting Foreman tire himself out by throwing punch after punch while my uncle leaned back against the ropes, absorbing the blows. It was a risky strategy that demanded physical endurance and incredible mental strength. He had to trust his plan, even as the world thought he was losing.

As the rounds went on, something incredible happened. Foreman began to slow down, his punches losing their power. And that's when my uncle made his move. He unleashed a series of quick, powerful punches, knocking Foreman to the canvas in the eighth round. The crowd erupted, and my uncle had done it—he had reclaimed the heavyweight title in one of the most iconic fights in history.

The lesson in that victory wasn't just about boxing. It was about life. My uncle showed me that mental barriers are often the hardest to overcome but also the most crucial. The mind is where the battle is won or lost. It's the voice in your head that tells you to keep going when everything else in you wants to stop.

In my own journey, there have been countless times when I've hated the training—when the pain seemed too much when the setbacks felt overwhelming. But in those moments, I remember my uncle's words: "Suffer now and live the rest of your life as a champion." I realize that those moments of suffering are the very things that build you up and prepare you for the challenges ahead.

Prophetic Word on Overcoming Mental Barriers

The Lord is speaking to you today about the barriers in your mind that have held you back. These barriers—whether they be fears, doubts, or limiting beliefs—are not too significant for God to overcome. I hear the Lord saying, "Do not allow these thoughts to define you or to dictate your path. I have not given you a spirit of fear but of power, love, and a sound mind."

God's grace is sufficient for you, even in your moments of weakness. He says, "My power is made perfect in your weakness. Where you see a barrier, I see an opportunity for My strength to shine through you." It is time to confront those limiting beliefs with the truth of God's word and the affirmation of who He has created you to be.

The Lord is calling you to rise above the mental barriers and to declare His promises over your life. As you write down those fears and replace them with positive affirmations, you are not just speaking words—you are aligning your mind with the truth of God's word.

The Lord says, "I am with you in this battle of the mind. These barriers will not defeat you. As you trust in Me and My grace, you will find the strength to push through, persevere, and emerge as the champion I have called you to be."

It is your season to break free from the chains of fear and limitation. God's grace is your empowerment, and His truth is your weapon. Stand firm, knowing that He who began a good work in you will carry it on to completion.

For those of you reading this, I want you to know that it's okay to hate the grind sometimes and feel like quitting. But it's in those moments that you need to push through. Identify the mental barriers holding you back, whether fear, doubt or the voice that says you're not good enough. Write them down, and then write a positive affirmation to counter them. Remind yourself that the pain, the struggle, the hard work—it's all part of the journey to becoming a champion in whatever you're pursuing.

> **Prayer:** Heavenly Father, thank You for the strength You provide in our moments of weakness. As we face and overcome the mental barriers that hold us back, help us to rely on Your grace, knowing that it is sufficient for every challenge we encounter. Fill us with courage, a renewed sense of purpose, and let us walk boldly in the truth of who You've created us to be. Guide our thoughts and hearts to align

with Your will as we move forward. In Jesus' name, Amen.

Task: Identify one limiting belief or fear that's holding you back. Write it down, and then write a positive affirmation to counter it.

Notes

Day 12: Stay Focused

Ali's Quote: *"Champions aren't made in gyms. Champions are made from something they have deep inside them—a desire, a dream, a vision."*

Scripture: *"Whatever you do, work at it with all your heart, as working for the Lord, not for human masters."* - Colossians 3:23

Prayer: Heavenly Father, keep the reader focused on their goal. May they work diligently and wholeheartedly, knowing they serve You in all they do. Amen.

Stay Focused – My Journey

As I sat quietly in my room, I found myself reflecting on my journey. Being Muhammad Ali's nephew has always been both an honor and a challenge, with expectations constantly looming over me. But today, I wasn't focused on what others expected of me; I focused on the truth of who I was in God's eyes and the vision He had placed in my heart.

Growing up, I often heard people tell me what I should be, how I should act, and what I should aspire to achieve. The shadow of my uncle's greatness loomed large, and for years, I tried to mold myself to fit the expectations of the world around me. But I realized that champions aren't made by conforming to others' expectations—they are forged by the fire of desire, dreams, and vision deep within.

One evening, while training for a crucial fight, I found myself alone in the gym. My trainer had stepped out, leaving me with my thoughts. As I punched the heavy bag, frustration grew within me. Why was I doing this? Was it for myself or to live up to a legacy? I felt weighed down by the burden of expectations.

In that solitary moment, I remembered a verse from Colossians 3:23: "Whatever you do, work at it with all your heart, as working for the Lord, not for human masters." It struck me that my efforts needed to be focused not on pleasing others but on fulfilling the vision God had given me. The desire, the dream, the vision—it wasn't something imposed from the outside but something that God had planted deep within me.

I knelt in the middle of the gym and prayed. "Dear God, help me to see the truth of who I am and stay focused on the vision You've given me. Show me the path You have for me, not the path others expect me to take."

As I prayed, a profound sense of peace washed over me. I felt God's presence and heard a gentle whisper in my heart, "You are my beloved son. You are free to be who I created you to be. Stay focused on the vision I've given you, and I will guide your steps."

From that day forward, my perspective changed. I no longer trained to meet others' expectations but to honor the gifts and talents God had given me. I embraced my identity, not just as Muhammad Ali's nephew, but as Ibn Ali, a man with his own unique purpose and destiny fueled by a vision from God.

The freedom I found in embracing my true identity and focusing on my God-given vision allowed me to excel not just in the ring but in every aspect of my life. I realized that true greatness wasn't about meeting the world's standards but about living authentically and working wholeheartedly towards the vision God had placed in my heart.

One particularly powerful moment came during a community outreach event. I was speaking to a group of young men struggling with their identities and goals. As I shared my story, one young man, Jason, approached me afterward. He told me how he had been trying to live up to his father's expectations of becoming a lawyer, even though his true passion was art.

Jason's eyes were filled with uncertainty and fear of disappointing his family. I shared with him how I had faced similar struggles and how focusing on my God-given vision had set me free. "Jason," I said, "God has a unique purpose for each of us. You don't have to fit into a mold created by others. Stay focused on the vision God has given you, and you'll find true freedom and fulfillment."

That conversation changed Jason's life. He decided to pursue his passion for art, and over time, he became a successful artist, inspiring others through his work. Seeing him thrive in his true identity reinforced the message that living authentically in God's truth and staying focused on His vision is the path to greatness.

As I continue on my journey, I remain committed to the vision God has placed in my heart. I encourage you to do the same. Whatever goal or dream God has placed within you, work at it with all your heart, knowing that you are serving Him. Stay focused, stay true to the vision, and trust that God will guide you to greatness.

Reflection: As you continue your journey to greatness, remember that the desire, dream, and vision God has placed within you truly makes you a champion. Stay focused on the vision, work at it with all your heart, and trust God's guidance. The world may have its distractions, but your focus on God's purpose will lead you to victory.

Prophetic Word:

I declare that as you stay focused on the vision God has placed within you, distractions will fall away, and clarity will increase. You will find renewed strength and purpose as you work diligently towards your goal. The vision God has given you will lead you to greatness, and your life will inspire many to pursue their God-given dreams with passion and perseverance. Amen.

> **Prayer:** Heavenly Father, thank You for the vision and desire You've placed deep within our hearts. As we continue this journey, help us stay focused and committed to the goals You've called us to pursue. Remove distractions and give us the strength to work diligently with all our hearts, knowing that in everything we do, we are serving You. Keep our eyes fixed on the purpose You've set before us, and let our efforts glorify Your name. In Jesus' name, Amen.

Task: Set aside distraction-free time today to focus entirely on working towards your goal.

Notes

Day 13: Embrace Challenges

Ali's Quote: *"Don't count the days; make the days count."*

Scripture: *"Consider it pure joy, my brothers and sisters, whenever you face trials of many kinds, because you know that the testing of your faith produces perseverance."* - James 1:2-4

Prayer: Heavenly Father, help the reader embrace the challenges. May they grow in perseverance and find joy in every trial. Amen.

My Boxing Journey

I remember a time in my boxing career when I was faced with a challenge that tested not only my physical strength but also my mental resolve. Growing up as the nephew of Muhammad Ali, I was constantly reminded of the importance of perseverance and resilience. My uncle often said, "Don't count the days; make the days count." Those words echoed in my mind, especially during the most challenging moments in the ring. They reminded us that our challenges aren't just obstacles but opportunities to grow, learn, and become stronger.

One of the most significant challenges I faced was the lead-up to a crucial fight early in my career. My opponent was a seasoned fighter known for his power and relentless pressure in the ring. The stakes were high, and everyone was watching, waiting to see if I could live up to the Ali name. The pressure was immense, and the training was grueling.

During those weeks of preparation, I faced challenges that seemed insurmountable. There were days when my body felt like it couldn't take another round of sparring, my legs were fatigued, and my mind clouded with doubt. The training sessions were brutal, running at dawn, endless rounds on the heavy bag, and sparring with fighters who pushed me to my limits. Every day felt like a battle, not just against my opponent but against the voice in my head telling me to quit.

But then, I would hear my uncle's voice in my mind, reminding me, "Don't count the days; make the days count." I knew that every minute of pain, every drop of sweat, was an investment in my future, a step closer to victory. I remembered how my uncle had faced his own challenges in the ring, had been stripped of his title, faced fierce opponents, and yet always found a way to rise above it all. He didn't just fight the battles in the ring—he embraced them, using them as opportunities to prove his strength, his resilience, and his character.

One particularly tough day, after a punishing sparring session, I sat in the locker room, exhausted and questioning whether I had it in me to continue. My trainer, who had been with me from the start, saw the doubt in my eyes. He sat beside me and said, "Ibn, this is the moment that will define you. It's easy to keep going when everything is going your way, but it's in these moments—when you're tired, when you're hurting, when you want to quit—that champions are made. Don't count the days; make the days count."

His words hit me hard. I realized that this challenge, this fight, was my test. It was an opportunity to prove to myself and the world that I could push through the pain that I could overcome the obstacles in front of me. It was an opportunity to make every day, every training session, count.

From that moment on, I approached each day with renewed determination. I pushed through the pain, the fatigue, and the doubt. I embraced the challenges, knowing that they were shaping me into the fighter I was meant to be. I knew that each round of sparring, each mile I ran, was bringing me closer to victory.

When the night of the fight finally arrived, I was ready. I stepped into the ring not just as a fighter but as someone who had embraced every challenge and setback and used them to fuel my drive to succeed. My opponent was formidable, just as I had expected, but I was tougher. I remembered the countless hours of training, the moments when I wanted to quit but didn't, and I knew I could win.

As the fight progressed, I felt my confidence grow. I could see the impact of my preparation, how I moved, and how I reacted to my opponent's attacks. I wasn't just surviving the fight—I was dominating it. In the final round, I delivered a series of powerful punches that left my opponent reeling. With one final blow, I knocked him to the canvas. The referee's count seemed to last forever, but when it was over, I knew I had won.

That night, I proved to myself that I could overcome any challenge and rise above doubt and pain. I learned that challenges are not roadblocks but opportunities to grow, build character, and develop the perseverance needed to succeed.

James 1:2-4 reminds us, "Consider it pure joy, my brothers and sisters, whenever you face trials of many kinds, because you know that the testing of your faith produces perseverance."

For those of you reading this, I encourage you to embrace your challenges. Don't shy away from them, and don't let them defeat you. Instead, see them as opportunities to grow, strengthen your faith, and become the person God has called you to be. Remember, "Don't count the days; make the days count." Every challenge you face is a chance to do just that.

Reflection: As you continue this 40-day journey, know that every challenge you face is a chance to strengthen your faith and character. By embracing these moments and persevering, you make each day count and move closer to the person God created you to be. Let's rise to the challenges and make the most of every day.

Prophetic Word:

I declare that as you embrace the challenges before you, God will strengthen your resolve and empower you to overcome every obstacle. You will find joy in the trials, knowing that they refine your character and draw you closer to Him. Your perseverance will be a testimony to others, inspiring them to face their challenges with courage and faith. You are being prepared for greatness, and God's glory will be revealed in your life through your determination. Amen.

Prayer: Heavenly Father, help the reader to embrace the challenges before them. May they grow in perseverance and find joy in every trial. Amen.

BOOK TITLE

Task: Face a small challenge today that you've been avoiding. Take one step to overcome it.

BOOK TITLE

Notes

Day 14: The Will and The Skill

Ali's Quote: *"The will must be stronger than the skill."*

Scripture: *"But those who hope in the Lord will renew their strength. They will soar on wings like eagles; they will run and not grow weary; they will walk and not faint."* - Isaiah 40:31

Prayer: Heavenly Father, as the reader rests, renew their strength. May there be fortified in You, ready to take on the next phase of their journey. Amen.

Rest and Reflect – My Journey

I remember a pivotal moment in my life that reshaped my understanding of the balance between will and skill, growth and rest. It happened a few years ago when I was invited to speak at a youth conference. As I stood before hundreds of eager faces, I felt the weight of the responsibility I held. These young people looked up to me not just as Ibn Ali, Muhammad Ali's nephew, but as a mentor and a guide.

As I began to speak, I shared my journey, emphasizing the importance of having a will more substantial than the skill alone. I recounted the story of a young boxer named Jamal, a talented athlete with immense potential. Jamal had all the physical attributes of a champion, but he struggled with understanding the importance of balance—between pushing forward and taking the necessary time to rest and reflect.

Jamal was naturally gifted, but he approached life with an all-or-nothing mindset. He believed that his raw talent alone would carry him through any challenge. This perspective, however, began to crack when Jamal started to experience burnout. He trained relentlessly, often ignoring the signs that his body and mind needed rest. Jamal saw rest as a weakness, something that only the less dedicated embraced.

But then, Jamal faced a significant challenge—a fight against a seasoned opponent who had both skill and experience. Jamal's rigorous training had left him physically prepared but mentally and emotionally drained. When the fight began, he quickly realized that his will, though strong, was faltering because he had neglected to balance it with rest. His skill was evident, but he found himself struggling without the mental clarity and strength that comes from rest.

After the fight, which he narrowly won, Jamal was exhausted, not just from the physical exertion but from the mental and emotional toll it had taken on him. He reached out to me, seeking advice and guidance. I could see the weariness in his eyes, the frustration of knowing he wasn't performing at his best despite his hard work.

I shared with Jamal the wisdom I had learned over the years, much of it inspired by my uncle's teachings. "The will must be stronger than the skill," I told him, quoting my uncle. But I also added that for the will to be unyielding, it needs to be renewed and fortified—through rest, reflection, and time with God. I guided him to reflect on Isaiah 40:31: "But those who hope in the Lord will renew their strength. They will soar on wings like eagles; they will run and not grow weary; they will walk and not faint."

This scripture hit home for Jamal. It made him realize that true strength comes not just from relentless training but from taking the time to rest in God to renew his mind, body, and spirit. I encouraged him to take a step back, rest, and reflect on his journey so far, and allow himself to grow stronger from within.

Jamal took this advice to heart. He began to incorporate regular rest days into his training schedule—days where he would spend time in prayer, reflect on his goals, and simply allow his body to recover. Jamal learned that rest wasn't a sign of weakness but a critical part of building strength. His will became stronger as he rested, fortified by his faith and renewed energy.

Months later, when Jamal stepped back into the ring, he was a different fighter. He moved with confidence, not just because of his skill but because his will was stronger than ever. His opponents could sense the difference—the calm, focused energy from a fighter who knew the value of rest and reflection. He fought with a renewed determination, and it wasn't long before he started winning more convincingly, not just because of his physical prowess but because he had embraced the balance of will, skill, and rest.

Jamal's journey is a testament to the power of rest and reflection in the process of growth and maturity. It shows that no matter how strong our will or how great our skill is, we must take the time to renew ourselves, to reflect on our journey, and to find strength in God's presence.

Reflection: Take a moment to reflect on your journey. Are there areas in your life where you need to embrace rest and renewal? Ask God to help you find the balance between will and rest, and trust that He will guide you toward His perfect plan for your life.

As you continue this 40-day journey, remember that rest is not the absence of effort but the space where true growth and renewal happen. Take today to rest, reflect on what you've learned so far, and trust that God is strengthening you for the days ahead. He is with you every step of the way, renewing your will and fortifying your spirit for the challenges that lie ahead.

Prophetic Word:

To you, the reader, I share this prophetic word: God sees your efforts and desire to grow. He is calling you to embrace rest as part of your journey. Allow yourself to pause, reflect, and be renewed by His strength. You are not defined by how hard you push but by the balance you maintain in your life. God is guiding you towards a greater purpose, and as you rest in Him, your will and strength will be fortified for the journey ahead.

> **Prayer:** Heavenly Father, thank You for the gift of rest and renewal. As we take this time to pause and reflect on the journey so far, we ask that You refresh our spirits and strengthen our resolve. Help us to see the lessons we've learned and the progress we've made, and may we be renewed in Your strength as we prepare for the next phase of our journey. Let us trust in Your guidance and find peace in Your presence. In Jesus' name, Amen.
>
> **Task:** Take today to rest. Reflect on your journey so far and write down what you've learned.

Notes

Week 3: Deepening the Commitment

Day 15: The Power of Silence

Ali's Quote: *"Silence is golden when you can't think of a good answer."*

Scripture: *"Even a fool is thought wise if he keeps silent, and discerning if he holds his tongue."* - Proverbs 17:28

Prayer: Heavenly Father, grant the reader the wisdom to embrace the power of silence. May they speak thoughtfully and allow their words to reflect Your truth and love. Amen.

The Commitment

Growing up, I was often surrounded by voices that echoed the values of strength, determination, and resilience. Yet, one lesson took me years to understand fully—the power of silence. It's a lesson I want to share with you today because it has the potential to transform how you approach challenges and interactions in your life.

One day, I faced a situation that put this lesson to the test. I had just experienced a significant setback in my career, and the opinions and advice from those around me were overwhelming. Everyone had something to say, and I felt pressured to respond, defend myself, and explain my actions. But amidst the noise, a small voice inside urged me to remain silent.

I took a moment to step away from the chaos and found a quiet place to reflect. It was then that I remembered the words of Proverbs 17:28: "Even a fool is thought wise if he keeps silent and discerning if he holds his tongue." This scripture reminded me that silence could be a strength, a source of wisdom.

In that silence, I turned to prayer and sought God's guidance. I realized that not every situation demands an immediate response. Sometimes, the most powerful thing you can do is to pause, reflect, and allow God to speak to your heart. This doesn't mean avoiding confrontation or difficult conversations but approaching them with peace and purpose.

I noticed a change within myself as I embraced the power of silence. I became more attentive and empathetic, understanding the deeper issues at play. When I did speak, my responses were more thoughtful and impactful because they were rooted in prayerful consideration and a desire to reflect God's truth.

Silence became a powerful tool in overcoming challenges. When you face criticism, disappointment, or conflict, take a moment to be still. In that stillness, seek God's wisdom. Ask Him to guide your thoughts and words. You will find that this practice brings you peace and empowers you to navigate difficult situations with greater clarity and confidence.

In the moments of silence, may God will reveal His strength in you. He will give you the wisdom to speak words that build up and bring life. Your silence is not a sign of weakness but a testament to your trust in Him. As you practice this wisdom, you will become a beacon of hope and strength to those around you.

Reflection: Today, I encourage you to practice the wisdom of silence. When you can't think of a good answer, choose to pause. Let your silence be filled with prayer and reflection. And when you do speak, let your words reflect God's truth and love.

Remember, silence is golden because it creates space for God's voice to be heard in your heart and through your words. Trust in His guidance, and you will find the strength to overcome any challenge. God bless you on your journey.

Prophetic Word:

The Lord says, "In the stillness, I will speak to your heart. Do not rush to fill the silence, for it is in the quiet that I reveal My wisdom. In moments of challenge, pause and let My peace guide your thoughts. You allow Me to work on your behalf when you hold your tongue. Your words carry power—use them to bring life, not confusion. As you embrace silence, I will fill your spirit with discernment, and your voice will echo the truth and love that reflects My heart. Trust that I am moving and directing your steps in the quiet."

> **Prayer:** Heavenly Father, thank you for the gift of silence. In holding our tongue, may we hear you more clearly. May our hearts be filled with words of wisdom. We pray that you strengthen us in our challenges.

Task: Today, take a moment of silence before responding to any challenging situation. In that silence, pray for wisdom and guidance.

BOOK TITLE

Notes

Day 16: Practice Discipline

Ali's Quote: *"Only a man who knows what it is like to be defeated can reach down to the bottom of his soul and come up with the extra ounce of power it takes to win when the match is even."*

Scripture: *"No, I strike a blow to my body and make it my slave so that after I have preached to others, I myself will not be disqualified for the prize."* - 1 Corinthians 9:27

Prayer: Heavenly Father, grant the reader the discipline to overcome every obstacle. May they find the strength within themselves to persevere and win the prize. Amen.

A Story of Defeat and Discipline

I wasn't born when my uncle, Muhammad Ali, made the decision that would change the course of his life forever. But growing up in the Ali family, his story was more than just history—it was a legacy that shaped the way I understood discipline, sacrifice, and the cost of standing by one's convictions.

The year was 1967, and the Vietnam War was a subject of intense debate across the nation. My uncle, a man known for his courage both in and out of the ring, refused to be drafted into the military. He saw the war as unjust, and his beliefs led him to take a stand that few were brave enough to take. As a result, he was stripped of his heavyweight title, banned from boxing, and faced with losing his freedom. It was a crushing defeat, not just in the physical sense but in the eyes of the world.

Growing up, I often heard stories about this time in his life from family members who lived through it with him. They would describe how he went from being the most celebrated athlete in the world to being vilified and ostracized. But what struck me most was how my uncle handled that defeat. He didn't let it break him; instead, he used it to build a more profound discipline within himself.

Though I wasn't there to witness it firsthand, I've seen the impact that period had on him. My uncle would later reflect on those years, saying, "Only a man who knows what it is like to be defeated can reach down to the bottom of his soul and come up with the extra ounce of power it takes to win when the match is even." Those words weren't just about boxing—they were about life.

During the years when he was banned from boxing, my uncle didn't sit idle. He trained relentlessly, keeping his body and mind sharp, always preparing for the day he could return to the ring. He embodied the scripture from 1 Corinthians 9:27, where Paul speaks of striking a blow to his body and making it his slave so that he wouldn't be disqualified from the prize. My uncle knew that to regain his title, he would need more than physical strength—he would need the discipline to endure and rise again.

When he finally returned to the ring in 1970, the world saw a man who had been tempered by hardship and defeat. His discipline had carried him through the darkest days, allowing him to emerge as a champion and a symbol of resilience and perseverance.

Reflection: As you continue this 40-day journey to greatness, remember that discipline is the foundation of true success. Let it guide, strengthen, and inspire you to be a beacon of hope for others. You have the power to make a difference, one act of discipline at a time.

Prophetic Word

I say to you, the reader: Your defeats do not define you; your discipline does. In every challenge, there is an opportunity to reach down into the depths of your soul and find the strength to persevere. No matter what obstacles stand in your way, remember that you have the power to overcome them through the discipline of your mind, body, and spirit.

Prayer: Heavenly Father, I pray for each person reading this story. Grant them the discipline to overcome every obstacle in their life. May they find the strength within themselves to persevere, to strike a blow to their body and mind, and to win the prize that You have set before them. Amen.

Task: Identify one area where you need more discipline. Create a simple action plan to improve in that area.

Notes

Day 17: Adjust Your Plan

Ali's Quote: *"The man who views the world the same at fifty as he did at twenty has wasted thirty years of his life."*

Scripture: *"Many are the plans in a person's heart, but it is the Lord's purpose that prevails."* - Proverbs 19:21

Prayer: Heavenly Father, guide the reader in adjusting their plans according to Your will. May they be flexible and open to Your direction. Amen.

Making Adjustments

Reflecting on my uncle Muhammad Ali's life, one of the most powerful lessons he taught me was the importance of adjusting, adapting, and overcoming—especially in the face of unexpected challenges. My uncle was a man who didn't just survive adversity; he thrived in it, often emerging stronger and wiser. His ability to adapt, to adjust his plans, and to overcome seemingly insurmountable odds is a lesson that continues to resonate with me and, I hope, with you as well.

One of the most challenging times in my uncle's life was when he was stripped of his heavyweight title and banned from boxing for refusing to be drafted into the Vietnam War. At the peak of his career, in his prime, he was suddenly cut off from the sport he loved, from the glory and the success he had worked so hard to achieve. It wasn't just a loss of titles—it was a loss of identity, a stripping away of everything he had built.

But instead of allowing this setback to define him, my uncle chose to adapt and grow. He used the time away from boxing to strengthen his mind and spirit. He became a voice for justice, speaking out against war, racism, and inequality. He didn't let the world view him as a victim of circumstance; instead, he became a symbol of resistance and integrity.

When my uncle was finally allowed to return to the ring after three and a half years, he was older, and many believed his best years were behind him. But he adjusted his approach, knowing he couldn't rely solely on the physical abilities that had once made him unstoppable. He came back with a deeper understanding of the game, with more wisdom and a refined strategy. Muhammad Ali knew he wasn't the same fighter he had been at twenty-five and didn't try to be. Instead, he embraced the man he had become at thirty-two—wiser, more determined, and with a greater sense of purpose.

His return to the ring was nothing short of remarkable. He faced some of the most formidable opponents of his career during this period, including his legendary fights against Joe Frazier and George Foreman. These were fights that demanded not just skill but the ability to adapt, adjust in real-time, and outthink his opponents. My uncle showed the world that true greatness isn't just about physical prowess but mental and spiritual resilience. It's about the ability to change, grow, and overcome whatever life throws at you.

I remember asking my father about this time in my uncle's life, about how he managed to come back after such a long absence and still be a champion. My father told me, "Your uncle understood that life is always changing, that the world you see at twenty isn't the same at fifty. He knew that to stay the same, to refuse to grow and adapt, was to waste the years God gives us. He adjusted his plans and strategy, overcoming them because he was willing to change."

This lesson is one that I've carried with me throughout my life and career. I've learned that no matter how well you plan, life has a way of throwing curveballs. The key is to stay flexible, to be willing to adjust your plans according to the circumstances, and to trust that God's purpose will prevail, as Proverbs 19:21 reminds us: "Many are the plans in a person's heart, but it is the Lord's purpose that prevails."

For those of you reading this, I encourage you to take a moment to review your plans. Are there areas where you need to adjust and adapt in order to keep moving forward? Don't be afraid to change course if necessary. Growth comes from being open to new directions, from recognizing when it's time to let go of what no longer serves you, and embracing the wisdom that comes with experience. Remember, the man who views the world the same at fifty as he did at twenty has wasted thirty years of his life. Don't waste the time God has given you—use it to grow, learn, and become the person He created you to be.

Reflection: As you continue on this 40-day journey, remember that adjusting your plans is not a sign of failure but a mark of wisdom and maturity. Trust in God's purpose for your life and allow Him to guide you as you adapt and grow. Let's move forward with wisdom, determination, and the courage to embrace change.

Prophetic Word:

I declare that as you adjust your plans and embrace the changes in your life, God will give you the wisdom to navigate every challenge. He is guiding you, even when the path seems unclear. As you remain open to His direction, you will find strength and clarity, and your journey will lead you to a greater purpose than you could have imagined. God is with you, shaping you through every twist and turn, and you will emerge victorious, stronger, and wiser for having trusted in His plan. Amen.

Prayer: Heavenly Father, guide the reader in adjusting their plans according to Your will. May they be flexible and open to Your direction. Amen.

Task: Review your plan. Adjust timelines or goals as needed to stay on track without feeling overwhelmed.

BOOK TITLE

Notes

Day 18: Seek Inspiration

Ali's Quote: *"Live every day as if it were your last because someday, you're going to be right."*

Scripture: *"Teach us to number our days, that we may gain a heart of wisdom."* - Psalm 90:12

Prayer: Heaven Father, inspire the reader to live each day with purpose and passion. May they seek wisdom in every moment and live in a way that honors You. Amen.

Inspiration

I remember a moment from my childhood that profoundly impacted me, a memory that has stayed with me throughout my life. It was a time when I sought inspiration, though I didn't fully realize it at the moment. I was just a boy trying to understand what it meant to carry the Ali name and what it meant to live up to the legacy of my uncle, Muhammad Ali. This memory has been a source of strength and inspiration for me.

I was around eight years old when it happened. My family had gathered at my uncle's house for a big family dinner. Everyone was there—my cousins, aunts, uncles, and, of course, my uncle, Muhammad Ali. The house was alive with laughter, conversation, and the delicious smells of food cooking in the kitchen. But as the evening wore on, I found myself feeling a little overwhelmed by it all. Being Muhammad Ali's nephew was something people always reminded me of, and even at that young age, I felt its weight.

After dinner, I slipped away from the crowd and wandered down to the basement, where my uncle often retreated to find some peace and quiet. The basement was a simple room filled with old boxing memorabilia, books, and a few pieces of exercise equipment. It was a place where my uncle could be himself, away from the spotlight.

As I walked down the stairs, I saw him sitting there, alone, resting in a big, comfortable chair. He looked up as I entered the room and smiled, that famous Ali smile that could light up a room. "Hey, champ," he said softly, using the nickname he often called me. "What's on your mind?"

I hesitated momentarily, unsure how to put my feelings into words. "Uncle Muhammad," I finally said, "do you ever get tired of being the greatest?"

He looked at me for a long moment as if weighing the question in his mind. Then, with a gentle chuckle, he patted the seat next to him, inviting me to sit down. "Come here, Ibn," he said. "Let me tell you something."

I sat down next to him, and he put his arm around my shoulders, pulling me close. "You know, everyone calls me the greatest," he began, his voice calm and reflective. "But the truth is, I'm not the greatest. You are."

I looked up at him, confused. "Me?" I asked. "But you're the one who won all those fights, who stood up for what you believed in, who everyone looks up to."

He nodded, smiling at my words. "That's true," he said. "But being great isn't just about winning fights or being famous. It's about living every day as if it were your last, making the most of your time, and finding the wisdom to live in a way that honors God and the people around you."

Then he reached over to a nearby bookshelf, his hand lingering over a collection of well-worn books, and pulled out a small, beautifully bound volume. He handed it to me with a serious expression. "This is a book by a Muslim scholar, Al-Ghazali," he said. "It's called *The Alchemy of Happiness*. This book has been a source of inspiration for me. It reminds me of the importance of living a life of purpose, seeking wisdom in every moment, and making each day count."

He opened the book to a passage he had bookmarked and read aloud: "The happiness of this world lies in the understanding of the transience of worldly pleasures and in the pursuit of the eternal happiness that comes from the soul's alignment with God."

His words hit me hard, even as a young boy. I had always seen my uncle as larger than life, someone who could do no wrong. But at that moment, I realized that what made him truly great wasn't just his skill in the ring but the way he lived his life with purpose and passion, the way he sought wisdom and inspiration from various sources, including his faith.

As we sat in the quiet basement, my uncle continued to speak, his voice filled with warmth and love. "You have the potential to be great, Ibn," he said. "But greatness isn't something you achieve overnight. It's something you work on every day. It's about the choices you make, how you treat others, and how you live your life. Never forget that."

He hugged me then, holding me close for a long moment. "Remember, champ," he whispered, "I'm not the greatest—you are. You have the power to live a life that inspires others, just as you inspire me."

As I lay in bed that night, I thought about what my uncle had said and the book he had shared with me. I realized that seeking inspiration isn't just about looking up to others—it's about finding the strength and wisdom within yourself to live each day with purpose. It's about living in a way that honors God and the people around you and making everyday count.

For those of you reading this, I encourage you to seek inspiration in your own life. Find something that motivates you, whether it's a book, a podcast, or a conversation with someone you admire. Live each day as if it were your last and strive to gain a heart of wisdom in everything you do. Remember, the greatness you seek is already within you—embrace, nurture, and let it shine.

Reflection: As you continue this 40-day journey, remember that inspiration is all around you, waiting to be discovered. Seek it out, embrace it, and let it fuel your journey toward greatness. And never forget that the potential for greatness is within you—live each day with that knowledge, and you will also inspire others.

Prophetic Word:

I declare that as you seek inspiration in your life, God will reveal to you the wisdom and strength you need to live each day with purpose. You will find new sources of motivation and clarity, and your life will become a beacon of hope and inspiration for others. God is with you, guiding your steps and helping you to make every day count. Embrace the greatness within you and let His light shine through you. Amen.

Prayer: Heavenly Father, inspire the reader to live each day with purpose and passion. May they seek wisdom in every moment and live in a way that honors You. Amen.

Task: Find a book, podcast, or video that inspires you and spend time with it today to refuel your motivation.

Notes

Day 19: Overcome Fear

Ali's Quote: *"Fear is not real. The only place that fear can exist is in our thoughts of the future. It is a product of our imagination."*

Scripture: *"For God has not given us a spirit of fear, but of power and of love and of a sound mind." - 2 Timothy 1:7*

Prayer: Heavenly Father, remove the spirit of fear from the reader's heart. Fill them with Your power, love, and a sound mind to overcome any fears they face. Amen.

Overcoming Fear

In the prime of his career, Muhammad Ali was not just a boxer; he was a symbol of courage, confidence, and conviction. But behind the bold proclamations, the witty banter, and the seemingly unshakable confidence, there were moments when even The Greatest had to wrestle with fear.

One such moment came in the lead-up to his historic fight against Sonny Liston. Liston was a formidable opponent, a towering figure with a fearsome reputation. He was the reigning heavyweight champion, known for his brutal power and menacing demeanor. The world had already decided that Ali, still known as Cassius

Clay, stood no chance against him. The odds were stacked heavily against the young challenger.

As the fight day approached, the pressure mounted. Ali was bombarded with doubts from all sides. Pundits, fans, and even some of his closest confidants questioned whether he had bitten off more than he could chew. It wasn't just about winning or losing; it was about facing a man who many believed could end his career with one punch.

One night, alone in his training camp, Ali found himself overwhelmed by these thoughts. The bravado that had carried him through countless interviews and press conferences seemed to fade in the silence. The fear of losing and of being humiliated in front of the world began to creep in. He thought about the immense power of Liston, the way he had demolished his previous opponents, and the painful reality of what could happen if he failed.

But then, Ali remembered something his mother had told him when he was a child: "Fear is a liar. It only has power if you believe in it." He had faced fear before—whether it was the fear of growing up in a segregated America or the fear of stepping into the ring for the first time. Each time, he had chosen to stand tall and confront the fear head-on, and he had emerged stronger each time.

Ali got up from his bed, walked to the mirror, and looked at his reflection. "You're the greatest," he said to himself, not as a boast but as a reminder. "Fear is not real. It's just a thought, a shadow. But you? You're real. Your power, your skill, your heart—those are real."

With that, Ali planned. He would not let fear dictate his actions. Ali would not allow the shadow of doubt to cloud his mind. Instead, he would focus on what he knew to be true—his training, strategy, and will to win. He would fight not just to prove the world wrong but to prove to himself that fear had no place in his life.

The following day, Ali's demeanor had changed. He walked into the gym with a renewed sense of purpose, his confidence radiating. He trained harder and pushed himself further, and when he stepped into the ring against Sonny Liston, he was ready.
The fight that followed became one of the most iconic moments in sports history. Ali danced around the ring, taunting Liston and defying expectations with speed, agility, and precision. Liston, the feared champion, couldn't keep up. In the seventh round, Liston didn't come out of his corner. The fight was over. Muhammad Ali

was the new heavyweight champion of the world.

As Ali stood victorious in the center of the ring, he knew that the real battle had been won long before the first punch was thrown. It had been won in that quiet moment in his training camp when he had chosen to confront his fear, to acknowledge it, and then to move past it.

Ali's victory that night was more than just a triumph of skill; it was a triumph of spirit. It was a testament to the truth that fear is nothing more than a shadow, powerless unless we give it form. By refusing to let fear control him, Ali had not only defeated Sonny Liston—he had defeated the doubts and fears that sought to hold him back.

To those who face their fears today, Ali's story serves as a powerful reminder: Fear is not real. It exists only in the thoughts of the future, a product of our imagination. The true power lies within you—within your heart, your mind, and your will to overcome. Stand tall, face your fears, and let your faith guide you to victory, just as it did for The Greatest.

Prophetic Word:

Beloved, the Lord sees the fears that weigh upon your heart, the doubts that whisper in the quiet moments, and the uncertainty that tries to shake your resolve. But today, He is calling you to rise above those fears. For He has not given you a spirit of fear, but of power, love, and a sound mind.

The Lord says, "Do not be afraid, for I am with you. The very thing you fear is a shadow, and My light will expose it for what it truly is—powerless in the presence of My strength within you. Take heart and take action, for I am guiding you in your steps. As you confront this fear, even in the smallest way, you will find that My grace is sufficient for you, and My power is made perfect in your weakness."

Today, as you write down that fear, know that you are not alone in this journey. Heaven stands with you, and as you take that small step to confront what has held you back, you will begin to see the chains of fear break. The Lord empowers you to move forward with courage, face the challenges ahead with confidence, and walk in the fullness of the destiny He has prepared for you.

You are more than a conqueror through Christ who loves you. This step, however small it may seem, is a mighty act of faith that will open doors to more significant victories. Trust in the Lord's strength and watch as He turns your fears into stepping-stones for your journey. In Jesus' mighty name, Amen.

> **Prayer:** Heavenly Father, thank You for reminding us that fear has no place in the hearts of

Your children. As we confront the fears that try to hold us back, we ask for Your power, love, and wisdom to fill us completely. Strengthen our hearts and minds so we can face every challenge with boldness and faith. Help us to walk in the confidence that You are always with us, guiding and protecting us. Let Your peace replace all fear as we trust in Your perfect plan. In Jesus' name, Amen.

Task: Write down a fear you have about your journey. Take one small step today to confront it.

BOOK TITLE

Notes

Day 20: Strengthen Your Support System

Ali's Quote: *"I am the greatest. I said that even before I knew, I was."*

Scripture: *"As iron sharpens iron, so one person sharpens another."* - Proverbs 27:17

Prayer: Heavenly Father, strengthen the reader's relationships with those who support and uplift them. May the reader find encouragement and growth in their community. Amen.

Strong Support Systems

Reflecting on my journey, one of the most powerful lessons I've learned is the importance of surrounding myself with people who believe in me—people who see my potential even when I struggle to see it myself. My uncle, Muhammad Ali, had a way of speaking greatness into existence. He famously declared, "I am the greatest," long before the world acknowledged his greatness. This boldness wasn't born from arrogance but from a deep-seated belief in his purpose and the support of those around him who sharpened his resolve.

In my life, I've been blessed with mentors and friends who have played a crucial role in shaping me into the person I am today. One such person was my coach, who saw potential in me before I stepped into the ring. He was there during the long hours of training,

pushing me beyond my limits and reminding me of the greatness that lay within me, even when I was too tired to believe it myself.
There was a time when I was preparing for a fight that felt like more than just a match—it was a defining moment in my life. The pressure was immense, and the fear of failure was almost paralyzing. I remember sitting in the locker room, my hands wrapped and ready, but my mind was anything but prepared. I felt alone at that moment despite the crowd cheering outside.

But then, my coach walked in. He didn't say much at first; he just sat beside me. After a few moments of silence, he said something I'll never forget: "You are greater than this fight. This is just one moment in a life full of victories. But right now, you need to believe in that greatness." His words echoed my uncle's confidence in himself, which had been sharpened by the people who believed in him.

My coach didn't just train my body; he sharpened my spirit. He reminded me that greatness isn't just about winning; it's about believing in the journey and the people who walk it with you. His encouragement gave me the strength to push past my fears and step into that ring with a renewed sense of purpose.

That fight wasn't just a test of my physical strength but a testament to the power of a strong support system. Just like iron sharpens iron, the people in our lives sharpen us, molding us into stronger, more resilient versions of ourselves. I won that fight, but more importantly, I learned that I am never alone in this journey. The strength of those who believe in and support us is immeasurable.

Prophetic Word:

To the reader, I want to share this prophetic word: You are surrounded by greatness, not just within yourself, but in the people God has placed in your life. As you continue your journey, remember that you are being sharpened by those who walk with you. Seek out those relationships, nurture them, and allow them to shape you into the person you are meant to be. You are not alone, and with the support of others, you will achieve the greatness within you. Be bold, be courageous, and know that your most incredible days are ahead, sharpened by the iron of those who believe in you.

As you reach out to those who have positively influenced your journey today, may you find renewed strength and encouragement. Thank them for their role in your life, and allow their wisdom to guide you forward. Remember, just as iron sharpens iron, so too will your relationships sharpen your spirit.

> **Prayer:** Heavenly Father, thank You for the people You have placed in our lives to uplift, support, and sharpen us. As we continue this journey, help us strengthen these relationships and seek wise counsel. May we always be grateful for

those who pour into us, and may we also be a source of encouragement to others. Surround us with a community that reflects Your love and helps us grow into the people You have called us to be. In Jesus' name, Amen.

Task: Reach out to a mentor or friend who has positively influenced your journey. Thank them and ask for advice or encouragement.

BOOK TITLE

Notes

Day 21: Rest and Reflect

Ali's Quote: *"A man who has no imagination has no wings."*

Scripture: *"Be still and know that I am God; I will be exalted among the nations, I will be exalted in the earth."* - Psalm 46:10

Prayer: Heavenly Father, grant the reader a moment of stillness to reflect on their journey. May they find peace in Your presence and gain clarity for the road ahead. Amen.

A Moment of Stillness

Sometimes in life, the most powerful thing we can do is to simply be still. We find clarity, strength, and guidance in the stillness to move forward. As I reflect on my journey, I'm reminded of a day that changed my perspective on the importance of rest and reflection.

It was a few years ago, during a particularly challenging season in my life. I had been pushing myself relentlessly, trying to meet every expectation and achieve every goal. My mind was constantly racing, my body was exhausted, and my spirit felt weighed down by the pressures I was facing. Despite my efforts, I felt like I was losing my way, like I was on a treadmill, running fast but going nowhere.

One afternoon, I found myself at a quiet park near my home after a long day. The sun was setting, casting a warm glow over the landscape, and the world around me seemed to pause. I sat down on a bench, feeling the weight of my burdens pressing on my shoulders. For the first time in a long while, I allowed myself to just be still.

As I sat there, I heard the gentle rustling of the leaves in the breeze and the distant sound of birds singing their evening song. The tranquility of the moment began to seep into my soul, and I felt a sense of peace that I hadn't experienced in a long time. In that stillness, I realized how much I had been striving without genuinely reflecting. I had been so focused on the destination that I had forgotten the importance of the journey.

At that moment, a scripture came to mind: "Be still and know that I am God" (Psalm 46:10). It was as if God was speaking directly to me, reminding me that He was in control, that I didn't have to carry the weight of the world on my own. I felt His presence in a way that I hadn't felt in a long time, bringing me to a place of surrender. I knew then that I needed to rest, reflect, and realign my focus with His purpose for my life.

During that time of reflection, I began to see my challenges in a new light. They were no longer obstacles but opportunities for growth. I started to imagine new possibilities, paths I hadn't considered before because I was too busy to see them. My imagination began to take flight, giving me wings to rise above my circumstances.

As I continued to reflect in the following days, I made crucial changes in my life. I set aside time each day for quiet reflection, to be still and listen to God's voice. I learned to trust in His timing, let go of the need to control everything and allow His peace to guide my steps.

That season of stillness became a turning point in my life. It was in the quiet moments that I found the strength to move forward with a renewed sense of purpose and direction. The rest and reflection I allowed myself gave me the clarity I needed to pursue my dreams with greater focus and determination.

Prophetic Word

Today, I speak a prophetic word over you: May you find peace in the stillness and may God's presence bring clarity to your heart. As you rest and reflect, may your imagination be renewed, giving you wings to soar above any challenge. Trust in His timing, for He guides you on a path of purpose and fulfillment. You are not alone; God is with you every step of the way. Amen.

Prayer: Heavenly Father, thank You for the gift of stillness and reflection. As we pause today, help us to find peace in Your presence and to recognize how You have guided us thus far. Renew our minds, hearts, and open our eyes to the possibilities that lie ahead. May our imagination be inspired by Your vision for our lives, and may we trust You with every step of the journey. Fill us with clarity, peace, and confidence as we move forward in faith. In Jesus' name, Amen.

Task: Spend time quietly reflecting today. Consider how your imagination has shaped your journey so far.

Notes

Week 4: Solidifying the Change

Day 22: Embrace the New You

Ali's Quote: *"I know where I'm going and I know the truth, and I don't have to be what you want me to be. I'm free to be what I want."*

Scripture: *"Therefore, if anyone is in Christ, the new creation has come: The old has gone, the new is here!"* - 2 Corinthians 5:17

Prayer: Heavenly Father, help the reader to embrace their new identity in You. May they walk confidently in the transformation You have brought into their life. Amen.

Becoming the New You

As I reflect on my journey, I am reminded of the countless battles I've faced. Some were against formidable opponents in the ring, but the most challenging battles were the ones within me. The quote, "My toughest opponent has always been me," resonates deeply with me because it captures the essence of my greatest struggles. Yet, those struggles were not in vain—they were the very fires that forged the new me.

Growing up, I was surrounded by the legacy of greatness. My uncle, Muhammad Ali, was a living legend whose achievements set a high bar. But as I came into my own, I realized that my path was not about living up to someone else's legacy. It was about becoming who I was meant to be. The most challenging battles were not against external expectations but within my heart and mind. In these internal arenas, I discovered the true meaning of transformation and faith.

There were times when doubt and fear gripped me, making it difficult to move forward. I remember one particular instance when I was preparing for a crucial fight. Physically, I was in peak condition, but mentally, I was struggling. The fear of failure loomed large, and I questioned my abilities. In these moments, I turned to God for strength and guidance, seeking the courage to embrace the new me that was emerging from the old.

Romans 7:15 speaks to our internal conflict: "I do not understand what I do. For what I want to do I do not do, but what I hate I do." This scripture resonated deeply because it articulated the battle between my desires and actions. I wanted to be courageous and confident, but I often succumbed to fear and self-doubt. But these struggles were a necessary part of the process—part of shedding the old and stepping into the new creation God called me to be.

I sought God's wisdom in the quiet moments of prayer and reflection. I asked Him to help me understand my struggles and to give me the strength to overcome them. Through this process, I began to see that my greatest opponent was not the person standing across from me in the ring but the old version of myself that I needed to leave behind. The doubts, fears, and insecurities that once held me back were the things that God was helping me overcome so that I could step into the new me He was creating.

One night, as I lay in bed, I felt a sense of peace; I felt God's presence and heard His gentle whisper: "You are not alone. I am with you. The new you is emerging." This prophetic word filled me with hope and courage. I realized that with God's help, I could overcome any challenge, no matter how insurmountable it seemed. I was no longer defined by the old me—the doubts, the fears, the insecurities. I was becoming someone new, someone stronger, someone who walked in alignment with God's will.

From that moment on, I approached my training and life with a renewed sense of purpose. I committed to aligning my actions with God's will, seeking His guidance in every decision. The transformation was not immediate, but with each passing day, I grew stronger and more confident in the new identity that God was forming within me. I learned to silence the negative voices in my head and focus on the positive, uplifting truths God spoke over my life. I was no longer battling to maintain the old—I embraced the new me with confidence and joy.

As you read this story, I want you to know that you, too, can become the new you. Your struggles are not meant to defeat you but to refine you. With God's help, you can conquer the fears and doubts that hold you back and step into the new creation He has destined you to be. Reflect on the areas of your life where you struggle the most and commit to seeking God's guidance and strength. Embrace the new you that God is calling forth.

Believe that with His help, you can overcome any challenge. Remember, you are not alone. God is with you, and He will never leave you or forsake you. Embrace His strength and let it empower you to live victoriously as the new you, He has created.

Prophetic Word:

I declare that you will find the strength to embrace the new you that God is forming within you. The old is gone, and the new is here. God is with you, and He will guide you through every challenge. You are destined for greatness; with His help, you will achieve more than you ever thought possible. Be encouraged, for the Lord is your strength and your shield, and the new you are emerging victorious.

Celebrate who you are becoming.

> **Prayer:** Heavenly Father, thank You for the transformation You are working in our lives. As we step into the new creation You have called us to be, help us fully embrace our identity in Christ. Let us walk confidently in the changes You've made within us, trusting in Your purpose and plan for our lives. Strengthen our faith as we continue to grow and reflect Your love and truth. May we never look back but press forward into the fullness of who You've created us to be. In Jesus' name, Amen.

Task: Write down the changes you've noticed in yourself since starting this journey.

Notes

Day 23: Keep Going

Ali's Quote: *"It's not the mountains ahead to climb that wear you out; it's the pebble in your shoe."*

Scripture: *"Let us not become weary in doing good, for at the proper time we will reap a harvest if we do not give up."* - Galatians 6:9

Prayer: Heavenly Father, give the reader the endurance to keep going, even when the journey is challenging. May they trust in Your timing and not grow weary in doing good. Amen.

Never Give Up: Keep Going

The room was quiet, the only sound coming from the steady hum of the air conditioner. I sat across from my father, Rahman, as he carefully wrapped his hands with a roll of gauze. It was a ritual he had performed countless times before, a preparation that went beyond the physical act. Today, though, he wasn't preparing for a fight; he was preparing to share a story—one that I had asked him to recount many times but never grew tired of hearing.

"Tell me about the fight, Dad," I said, my voice filled with anticipation. "The one where Uncle Muhammad had that injury."

My father smiled, a gentle, knowing smile that spoke of years spent by his brother's side. He nodded slowly and leaned back in his chair, his eyes drifting to a place far from our small living room, back to a night when the world watched with bated breath.

"It was a big night," he began, his voice steady and calm. "Your Uncle Muhammad was getting ready to step into the ring again, but there was something different about this fight. He had a small injury, a pain in his foot that had started as nothing more than a little irritation. A pebble in his shoe, he called it. But that small pain grew as the day of the fight got closer. It wasn't enough to keep him out of the ring, but it was enough to worry me."

I watched my father closely, imagining him sitting ringside that night, the tension palpable as he waited for the fight to begin. I could almost see the worry etched into his face, feel the unease that must have settled in his chest.

"As the fight started," my father continued, "I could see that the pain was affecting him. His movements weren't as smooth as they usually were. Every step he took seemed to remind him of that pebble in his shoe, but he kept going. He wouldn't let it stop him. He knew what was at stake and wasn't about to let something so small hold him back."

My father paused as if reliving the moment in his mind before continuing. "The rounds went by, and your uncle kept fighting. But with each round, it became clearer that he was struggling. His jabs were slower, and his footwork was less precise. The crowd could see it, too. There was a murmur, a kind of collective uncertainty. But I knew your uncle. I knew that he wasn't just fighting his opponent in the ring—he was fighting against the pain, against the urge to give in."

I leaned closer, captivated by the story. "What happened next?"

My father's eyes softened as he recalled the pivotal moment. "In the final round, with just seconds left on the clock, your uncle did something extraordinary. He dug deep, deeper than I'd ever seen before. He found a reserve of strength that only someone like him could tap into. He let loose a series of punches that took everyone by surprise, including his opponent. The bell rang, and the crowd erupted. Your uncle had won, not just the fight, but the battle against that pebble in his shoe."

He looked at me then, his expression serious, the lesson clear in his eyes. "You see, son, your uncle understood something that most people forget. Galatians 6:9 says, 'Let us not become weary in doing good, for at the proper time we will reap a harvest if we do not give up.' That night, your uncle showed the world that it's not the mountains ahead that wear you out—it's the pebble in your shoe. But if you keep going, trust in God's timing, and don't give up, you can overcome even the toughest challenges."

I sat back, the weight of the story settling over me. My uncle Muhammad had always been a hero to me, but hearing my father recount that night made me see him in a new light. It wasn't just his strength or skill that made him great—it was his perseverance and refusal to let even the most minor obstacle keep him from achieving his goals.

As my father finished wrapping his hands, he lifted his eyes and smiled. "Remember this story, son. Life will throw pebbles in your path. Some will be so small you might not notice them initially, but they can grow if you let them. Don't let them stop you. Keep going, keep trusting, and in due time, you'll reap your harvest."

I nodded, the words sinking deep into my heart. I knew I would always carry this lesson with me, a reminder that even when the journey is arduous, I must keep going—just like my uncle Muhammad did on that unforgettable night.

Prophetic Word on Perseverance

In this moment, the Lord is speaking to you about the importance of perseverance in your journey. He sees the "pebbles" in your path—those small, nagging obstacles that try to wear you down and make you feel like giving up. But I hear the Lord saying, "Do not be discouraged by these small things, for they are not meant to stop you, but to strengthen you."

The Lord is calling you to identify these pebbles, not as a source of frustration but as an opportunity to grow in endurance. Just as the scripture in Galatians 6:9 encourages, you are called to keep doing good, to keep moving forward, and to trust that the harvest will come in due time if you do not give up.

God is saying, "My child, I am with you every step of the way. I see your obstacles, and I am giving you the strength to overcome them. Do not let these small things rob you of your focus or joy. Instead, take action to remove them and continue on the path I have set before you."

As you remove these pebbles, you will find that the journey becomes lighter and your steps more confident. The Lord equips you with the tools to persevere and keep going even when the path is challenging. Trust in His timing and know that every step of endurance brings you closer to fulfilling His promises for your life.

> **Prayer:** Heavenly Father, thank You for the strength and endurance You provide in times of challenge. As we continue on this journey, help us to recognize the small obstacles that may

hinder our progress and give us the wisdom and courage to overcome them. Renew our spirit and remind us of Your promise that, in due time, we will see the fruit of our labor if we do not give up. Guide us to keep going with faith, perseverance, and trust in Your perfect timing. In Jesus' name, Amen.

Task: Identify a small "pebble" or obstacle in your path. Take action to remove it today.

Notes

Day 24: Measure Your Success

Ali's Quote: *"If my mind can conceive it, and my heart can believe it—then I can achieve it."*

Scripture: *"I can do all this through him who gives me strength."* - Philippians 4:13

Prayer: Heavenly Father, as the reader measures their success, remind them that all things are possible through You. May they see the fruits of their labor and give You the glory. Amen.

Measure Your Success

I remembered those cherished moments with my Poppa Cash Clay, where I would nestle into the comforting embrace of my grandfather's lap. The old armchair creaked as Poppa settled in, his hands weathered but strong and his voice deep and rich with history.

"Let me tell you a story, little man," Poppa began, his eyes twinkling with a mix of nostalgia and pride. "It was a rainy night in Louisville back in '54. Your daddy was just 12 years old, but he'd already learned that life can be tough. You see, he had just gotten a brand-new red Schwinn bicycle, and he was as proud of that bike as you are of your favorite toy."

I could picture it vividly, the excitement of a young boy with a new bike, only to have it stolen away—a heartbreaking moment for anyone, let alone a child.

"Your dad was mad, Ibn, furious," Poppa continued, his voice taking on a serious tone. "He wanted to find whoever took that bike and give 'em a piece of his mind...and maybe his fists, too."

"But instead of going after the thief, he went looking for a man named Joe Elsby Martin," Poppa said, smiling as he recalled the wisdom of that decision. "Joe was a police officer who also ran a gym, a place where boys could learn to box and stay out of trouble. Your dad walked in there with tears in his eyes, telling Joe, "he wanted to 'whup' whoever stole his bike."

I listened intently, feeling the weight of the story. "Did he find the man who stole it, Poppa?" I asked, even though I knew the answer.

Poppa chuckled softly, shaking his head. "No, son, he didn't. But what he did find was something even more valuable. Joe looked at your dad and said, 'Before you start talking about whupping somebody, you'd better learn how to fight.' And that's exactly what your dad did. He learned how to fight, not just with his fists but with his heart and mind."

I felt pride as I imagined my young, determined father finding strength and purpose in that gym. The story was more than just a tale of a stolen bike; it was a lesson in resilience, discipline, and the power of channeling anger into something productive.

As Poppa finished the story, I snuggled closer, absorbing the warmth of my grandfather's love and the wisdom that came with it. I knew that these moments were the building blocks of who I was—stories of perseverance, belief, and the understanding that true success comes not just from achieving your goals but from the journey and the lessons learned along the way.

This memory, shared on his grandfather's lap, became a cornerstone for me, reminding me that success is measured not just by what you accomplish but by the strength you gain and the wisdom you acquire on the path to your dreams.

Prophetic Word

Dear reader, hear the word of the Lord. The time has come for you to rise above the limitations that have held you back. Though the seeds you have sown in faith may have been planted in tears, they are about to bear fruit in abundance. You have pressed on through the trials, and though the road has been long and weary, your perseverance has not gone unnoticed by the Almighty.

The Lord says, "I have seen your struggle, and I have heard your prayers. Know this: the breakthrough is at hand. What once seemed impossible will now be made possible through My strength within you. I am unlocking doors that no man can shut and opening pathways that have been hidden from you until this appointed time. You are stepping into a season of divine acceleration where what took years to build will now come together swiftly by My hand."

Do not fear the challenges that lie ahead, for I am with you. I have equipped you with everything you need to fulfill the purpose I have placed within you. The dreams and visions I have given you are not mere fantasies; they are My promises to you, and I am faithful to fulfill them.

As you measure your success, do not look only at the external victories but also the growth within your spirit. I am refining you, shaping you into a vessel of honor, prepared for every good work. The wisdom you have gained in the wilderness will be your strength in the promised land.

Prepare yourself, for I am about to pour out blessings upon you—blessings that will overflow into the lives of those around you. Your testimony will be a light in the darkness, a beacon of hope for those who are lost. You are called to be My witness, to show the world what is possible when a life is fully surrendered to Me.

Step forward in boldness and faith, knowing I am the God who goes before you. Your success is assured, not by your power, but by My Spirit, says the Lord. Be strong and courageous, for I am with you, and I will never leave you nor forsake you. Your time is now. Go forth and accomplish all I have destined for you, in Jesus' name. Amen.

> **Prayer:** Heavenly Father, thank You for the progress we've made and the strength You've given us along the way. As we measure our success, help us recognize Your hand in every achievement and give You all the glory. Guide us in setting new goals and continue strengthening our hearts and minds for the journey ahead. May we always trust in Your power to help us accomplish everything You've called us to. In Jesus' name, Amen.

Task: Take some time to measure the progress you've made. Acknowledge your achievements and set a new goal for the next phase.

Notes

Day 25: Rest but Never Quit

Ali's Quote: *"Rest but never quit. Even the sun has a sinking spell each evening. But it always rises the next morning. At sunrise, every soul is born again."*

Scripture: *"Because of the Lord's great love we are not consumed, for his compassions never fail. They are new every morning; great is your faithfulness."* - Lamentations 3:22-23

Prayer: Heavenly Father, thank You for Your mercies that are new every morning. Help me to find rest in You and to rise each day with renewed strength and hope. Amen.

Never Quit

When I was younger, I struggled with the weight of expectations and the shadows of doubt that often clouded my mind. The journey to greatness is not without its trials, and there were moments when the darkness seemed too overwhelming to overcome. But it was during these times that I learned the true power of resilience and the unwavering faithfulness of God.

There was a period in my life when everything seemed to be falling apart. I was dealing with personal losses, professional setbacks, and a sense of inadequacy that gnawed at my spirit.

Every evening, as the sun dipped below the horizon, I felt as though I too, was sinking into the abyss of my struggles. But each morning, as the first light of dawn broke through the darkness, I was reminded of the promise of a new beginning.

One particular morning stands out in my memory. The night before, I had been especially difficult, filled with restless sleep and a heart heavy with sorrow. But as I sat by the window, watching the sunrise, a profound sense of peace washed over me. It was as if the light was not just illuminating the world outside but also the depths of my soul. I realized then that, just as the sun rises each day, we, too, have the opportunity to rise anew, regardless of the challenges we face.

In those quiet moments of reflection, I turned to Lamentations 3:22-23, a passage that had always comforted me: "Because of the Lord's great love we are not consumed, for his compassions never fail. They are new every morning; great is your faithfulness." The words resonated deeply within me, reaffirming that God's love and compassion are constants in our lives, providing us with the strength to persevere.

From that day forward, I made a conscious decision to embrace each new day with hope and determination. I found solace in the knowledge that, no matter how difficult the previous day had been, the dawn of a new day brought the promise of renewed strength and opportunities. This mindset shift transformed my life, enabling me to face my challenges with a sense of purpose and resilience.

To you, dear reader, I share this prophetic word: You are not alone in your struggles. Just as the sun rises every morning, so too does God's mercy and compassion shine upon you. Each day is a gift, a chance to rise above your circumstances and step into the fullness of your potential. Do not be disheartened by the setbacks you encounter. Instead, see them as opportunities for growth and transformation.

Remember, rest is not a sign of weakness but a necessary pause to gather your strength. Quitting, however, is not an option. Even when the night seems darkest, hold on to the promise of the dawn. Trust in the faithfulness of God, who renews His mercies every morning and gives you the courage to face each day anew.

Embrace the journey with faith and hope, knowing you are continually being shaped and strengthened by the trials you overcome. Let the rising sun be a reminder of your resilience and the boundless love of your Creator. Rise each day with the confidence that you have the strength to conquer it no matter what comes your way.

Prophetic Word:

The Lord says, "My mercies are fresh for you with every sunrise. As the sun rises each morning, so too does My grace and compassion over your life. Do not fear the moments when you feel weary, for I am your source of strength. I will lift you up and renew your spirit. Though challenges may press upon you, I am making a way for you to rise again. Each day is a new beginning, filled with My favor and purpose. Trust that I am with you, guiding every step, and as you rest in Me, I will refresh and sustain you for the journey ahead. Do not quit, for I am faithful to complete the work I have started in you."

> **Prayer:** Heavenly Father, thank You for the gift of renewal You offer each day. As we rest in Your presence, help us to trust in Your faithfulness and embrace each morning with hope and determination. Strengthen us never to quit, even when challenges arise, and remind us that Your mercies are new every morning. Let Your love and compassion guide us forward, knowing that we can rise above every obstacle with You. In Jesus' name, Amen.

Task: Embrace each new day with hope and determination. Trust that God's mercies are renewed every morning; with each sunrise, you are given a fresh start to rise above your challenges.

BOOK TITLE

Notes

Day 26: Title: The Race of Faith

Ali's Quote: *"I'm so fast that last night I turned off the light switch in my hotel room and was in bed before the room was dark."*

Scripture: *"But those who hope in the Lord will renew their strength. They will soar on wings like eagles; they will run and not grow weary they will walk and not be faint."* - Isaiah 40:31

Prayer: Heavenly Father, renew my strength and give me the energy to run the race You have set before me. Help me trust Your timing and provision. Amen.

The Race of Faith

In my life, I have often found myself in situations where I had to rely on a strength greater than my own. There were times when the weight of my responsibilities, the pressure to perform, and the challenges of daily life felt overwhelming. But each time, I remembered the words of my uncle, Muhammad Ali, and the promises of God's Word.

One particular memory stands out to me. It was a few years ago, during a particularly challenging season of my life. I was preparing for an important event, one that required not just physical strength but also mental and emotional fortitude. The night before, as I lay in my hotel room, I couldn't shake off the anxiety. I remembered my uncle's humorous yet profound words about his speed. It reminded me that strength and speed are not just about physical abilities but also about the swiftness of faith and the power of trust in God.

As I turned off the light and lay in bed, I felt the darkness closing in. Yet, within that darkness, I felt a glimmer of hope. I closed my eyes and prayed, "Lord, renew my strength and give me the energy to run the race You have set before me. Help me trust Your timing and provision."

The following morning, I woke up with a renewed sense of purpose. Isaiah 40:31 echoed in my heart: "But those who hope in the Lord will renew their strength. They will soar on wings like eagles; they will run and not grow weary; they will walk and not be faint." I felt an inexplicable strength, not just physically but in my spirit. I knew that no matter what lay ahead, I could face it because my hope was in the Lord.

The event went better than I had anticipated. Each moment, I felt God's strength carrying me, helping me to overcome every challenge. It was not just my victory but a testament to the power of faith and the fulfillment of God's promises.

Dear reader, whatever race you are running today, whatever challenges you face, remember this: God is with you. He will renew your strength. You may feel like the darkness is overwhelming but know that even in the darkest times, God's light shines the brightest. You are not alone, and you never will be.

Prophetic Word:

I speak over your life today and tell you that you will experience a renewal of strength like never before. You will rise on wings like eagles, soaring above every obstacle. You will run and not grow weary, walk, and not be faint. Trust in the Lord, and He will guide you to victory.

May this journey be a source of hope and strength for you, and may you find encouragement.

> **Prayer:** Heavenly Father, thank You for the strength and endurance You provide as we run the race of faith. As we face challenges, help us lean on You for the strength to keep moving forward, knowing You are always with us. Renew our energy and guide us to trust in Your perfect timing and provision. May we run and not grow weary and walk without fainting because our hope is in You. In Jesus' name, Amen.

Task: Reflect on the story and the scripture. Write down a challenge you face and commit it to prayer, asking God to renew your strength and guide you through it. Trust in God's strength to help you overcome them. Believe in His promises and hold on to His Word. He will see you through.

BOOK TITLE

Notes

Day 27: Refine Your Goals

Ali's Quote: *"The best way to make your dreams come true is to wake up."*

Scripture: *"In their hearts, humans plan their course, but the Lord establishes their steps."* - Proverbs 16:9

Prayer: Heavenly Father, guide the reader as they refine their goals. May they wake up each day with renewed purpose and trust in the path You have set before them. Amen.

Refine Your Goals – My Journey with Coach Moses

As I reflect on my boxing career, one story always stands out when I think about refining goals and the importance of waking up each day with renewed purpose. It's a lesson I learned from my personal trainer, Moses, a man who had been with me through the highs and lows of my journey in the ring. He wasn't just a trainer; he was a mentor, a guide, and someone who knew how to push me to my limits while helping me refine my path.

It was a few years into my professional career, and I had been experiencing a series of wins that made me feel invincible. I was riding high, confident that everything I had set out to achieve was within my grasp. My goals were clear: I wanted to win titles, secure my legacy, and make my family proud. But as I continued to train and fight, something began to shift. My wins, while still satisfying, started to feel routine. The excitement I once felt before stepping into the ring faded, and the fire that had driven me began to wane.

Moses noticed this change in me before I even realized it myself. One morning, after an especially grueling training session, he called me over as I was about to leave the gym. His expression was serious, and I knew that whatever he was about to say would be significant.

"Ibn," he began, "you're doing well. You're winning, and you're strong, but I see something in you that worries me."

I was taken aback, "What do you mean, Moses? I'm winning. Isn't that what matters?"

He nodded slowly. "Winning is important, yes. But there's more to this journey than just victory. I've watched you grow, but I've also seen you start to settle. You're achieving your goals, but are those goals still pushing you? Are they still inspiring you to wake up every day with the same fire you had when you first started?"

I didn't have an answer for him. I hadn't thought about my goals in that way. I had set them early on and followed the plan I had created. But as I stood there, listening to Moses, I realized that my goals had become outdated somewhere along the way. They no longer reflected the person I was becoming or the new challenges I wanted to take on.

Moses must have sensed my uncertainty because he continued, "The best way to make your dreams come true is to wake up, Ibn. You've been on autopilot, doing what you've always done because it worked. But if you want to keep growing and reach new heights, you need to wake up and refine your goals. Make sure they challenge you and ignite that fire inside you."

He paused and then added, "Proverbs 16:9 says, 'In their hearts humans plan their course, but the Lord establishes their steps.' It's good to have plans, but you must be willing to adjust them to refine them as you grow. Trust that God is guiding you, but don't be afraid to change course if that's what's needed."

That conversation was a turning point for me. I went home that day and took a long, hard look at the goals I had set. I realized that while they had served me well initially, they no longer reflected the fighter—and the man—I wanted to be. I spent time praying, reflecting, and ultimately refining those goals. I set new challenges for myself, both in the ring and outside of it. I wanted to win titles and inspire others, be a role model, and use my platform to make a difference.

The next day, I entered the gym with renewed purpose. My training was no longer just about winning the next fight; it was about something bigger, something that truly motivated me to give my best every day. And that shift in mindset made all the difference. I fought with more passion, trained more intensely, and found a more profound joy in the journey.

For those of you reading this, I encourage you to take a moment to revisit your goals. Ask yourself if they still inspire you and reflect the person you are becoming. Don't be afraid to refine them; wake up and make the necessary adjustments that will keep you moving forward with purpose. Remember, as Proverbs 16:9 reminds us, it's crucial to plan, but it's even more important to trust in the path God has set before you.

As you continue this 40-day journey, know that refining your goals is not a sign of weakness but growth and wisdom. Embrace the changes, trust in God's guidance, and wake up each day ready to pursue the dreams that genuinely matter to you.

Prophetic Word:

I declare that as you refine your goals and align them with God's purpose for your life, you will find renewed strength and inspiration. God is guiding you to new heights, opening doors you never imagined, and leading you on a path of true fulfillment. Embrace this process of refinement, for it is shaping you into the person you are meant to be. Amen.

Prayer: Heavenly Father, guide the reader as they refine their goals. May they wake up each day with renewed purpose and trust in the path You have set before them. Amen.

Task: Revisit your goals and refine them based on what you've learned. Adjust your plan as necessary.

BOOK TITLE

Notes

Day 28: The Will to Win

Ali's Quote: *"Champions have to have the skill and the will. But the will must be stronger than the skill."*

Scripture: *"For it is God who works in you to will and to act in order to fulfill his good purpose."* - Philippians 2:13

Prayer: Heavenly Father, strengthen the reader's will and determination to pursue the goals You have set for them. Help the reader to rely on Your power and not just their abilities. Amen.

The Will to Win

Reflecting on my journey, the thing that stands out: the battles I faced were not won by skill alone. The strength of my will, fueled by faith, carried me through. I want to share a story that illustrates the power of will and determination, hoping it will inspire you to find the strength to overcome the challenges in your life.

A few years ago, I faced one of the most challenging seasons of my life. It wasn't in the ring but in my personal life. The business ventures I had poured my heart and soul into were crumbling. I faced financial stress, self-doubt, and a growing sense of failure. Every day felt like a battle against a formidable opponent, and I often questioned whether I had the strength to keep going.

One night, after a particularly grueling day, I found myself alone, sitting on the porch and staring into the night sky. The weight of my struggles felt overwhelming, and I wondered if I had reached my breaking point. In that quiet moment, I remembered a lesson my uncle, Muhammad Ali, had taught me: "Champions have to have the skill and the will. But the will must be stronger than the skill."

I realized that my will, determination, and faith were the keys to overcoming this challenge. I decided to lean into my faith more than ever, seeking God's strength to guide me through this storm. I started each day with prayer, asking God to work in me, as Philippians 2:13 says, to will and to act to fulfill His good purpose.

Gradually, I began to see changes. Doors that had seemed firmly shut began to open. New opportunities emerged, and I found the strength to persevere. It wasn't an overnight transformation but a gradual process of rebuilding my life, one step at a time. The challenges didn't vanish, but my perspective shifted. I no longer saw them as insurmountable obstacles but as opportunities to strengthen my faith and determination.

As I reflect on that season, I realize that it wasn't my skill that saw me through but the will to keep going, empowered by God's strength. This experience taught me that no matter the difficulty of the journey, we can overcome it with God's help.

To you, dear reader, I offer this prophetic word: God has placed within you strength more significant than any challenge you face. Trust in His power and let Him work through you to accomplish His purposes. Your will, strengthened by faith, can move mountains. Remember, champions are made by skill and the will to persevere.

This journey is about more than just overcoming challenges; it's about growing in faith, resilience, and determination. Embrace each day with the knowledge that you are not alone. God is with you, working in you to will and to act according to His good purpose. Let this be your source of hope and strength as you continue your journey to greatness.

Prophetic Word:

I sense a deep stirring within your spirit—a call to rise above the challenges that have weighed you down. Today, the Lord says to you, "Do not be discouraged by what you see before you. What appears to be a setback is a setup for something far greater than you can imagine. I am strengthening your resolve, sharpening your focus, and preparing you for a breakthrough that will astound even you. You have been chosen for a purpose that goes beyond your current understanding, and every trial you face is refining you, shaping you into the champion I have destined you to be."

"Trust in Me," says the Lord, "for I am with you in every step. I am the source of your strength, the author of your faith, and the finisher of your journey. The dreams I have placed in your heart are not there by accident. They are seeds of purpose, and I will bring them to fruition as you continue to walk in obedience and faith. Hold on to My promises, for they are sure and steadfast."

"Know this," declares the Lord, "your will, when aligned with My will, is unstoppable. I am infusing you with divine determination, a strength beyond human ability. What you have been through has not been in vain; it has prepared you for the victory that lies ahead. You are not just a survivor—you are an overcomer, a warrior in My Kingdom, and I have great things in store for you."

"Step forward confidently, knowing that I am working all things together for your good. You will see My hand in your life in ways you never expected. Keep your eyes on Me, and you will find the strength, the will, and the courage to overcome every obstacle.

Your story is not over; it is just the beginning. The best is yet to come."

Prayer: Heavenly Father, thank You for working in us to will and to act according to Your purpose. As we face challenges, help us to lean on Your strength, knowing that it is not by our skill alone but by the will and determination You've placed in us. Strengthen our resolve to pursue the goals You have set before us and guide us through every obstacle with Your power. May we trust You fully in all that we do. In Jesus' name, Amen.

Task: Reflect on a challenge you are currently facing. Write it down and pray over it. Ask God to strengthen your will and guide you in overcoming this obstacle with His power. Believe that with His help, you can overcome any obstacle.

Notes

Week 5: Achieving and Sustaining Change

Day29: Title: The Path of Service

Ali's Quote: *"The more we help others, the more we help ourselves."*

Scripture: *"Carry each other's burdens, and in this way, you will fulfill the law of Christ."* - Galatians 6:2

Prayer: Heavenly Father, teach the reader to serve others selflessly and to find joy in helping those in need. May their actions reflect Your love and compassion. Amen.

Ibn's Path of Service

As I embark on this 40-day journey to greatness, I'm reminded of a profound truth my uncle, Muhammad Ali, often spoke about the importance of serving others. The quote, "The more we help others, the more we help ourselves," has always resonated deeply with me. This principle has guided my life and inspired me to share this journey with you.

I recall a time when I was at a crossroads in my life. I felt lost, burdened by my own struggles, and unsure of how to move forward. During this period of uncertainty, I encountered a man named James. James was a humble janitor at a local community center, always seen sweeping floors and cleaning up after others. His life had been marked by hardship, but his spirit remained unbroken.

One day, I decided to strike up a conversation with James. He shared his story with me—of loss, resilience, and unwavering faith. Despite his challenges, James found joy in serving others. He told me he would stay late to help the children with homework, often buying them snacks with his meager earnings. His actions weren't grand gestures, but they significantly impacted the lives he touched.

Inspired by James' example, I volunteered at the community center. I began helping with various tasks, from organizing events to mentoring the youth. The more I served, the more I felt a sense of fulfillment and purpose. It was as if a weight had been lifted from my shoulders. I realized that in helping others, I was also healing myself.

One evening, a young girl approached me as I was leaving the center. She had been struggling with her studies and often felt overlooked at home. She shared how our time together gave her hope and confidence. Her words moved me deeply, and I knew then that my journey of service was not just about giving—it was also about receiving the blessings that came from lifting others.

This experience taught me a valuable lesson: we are all interconnected. Our actions, no matter how small, can create ripples of positive change. When we carry each other's burdens, we fulfill the law of Christ and strengthen our spirits. It's a cycle of love and compassion that enriches both the giver and the receiver.

As you walk this path of service, remember that your efforts matter. You have the power to make a difference in someone's life. It may be through a kind gesture, a listening ear, or simply being present for someone in need. Each act of service is a testament to the love of Christ working through you.

Prophetic Word:

I declare that as you step out in faith to serve others, you will experience a new level of joy and fulfillment. The Lord will bless the work of your hands and multiply your efforts. You will find strength in your challenges as you help others overcome theirs. Your life will be a shining example of God's love and compassion, inspiring those around you to do the same.

May this journey lead you to greatness, not just for yourself but for all those you touch along the way. Remember, the more we help others, the more we help ourselves. Let this truth guide you, and may you find hope and strength in every act of service.

Prayer: Heavenly Father, grant me the heart to serve others as You have served me with love, grace, and compassion. Open my eyes to see the needs around me and give me the strength and wisdom to act in ways that reflect Your glory. Let my hands and my words be instruments of Your kindness and truth, bringing comfort and hope to those in need. May every act of service point others to You, and may Your love be made visible throughout my life. In Jesus' name, Amen.

Task: Today, find someone in need and offer your assistance. Whether it's a kind word, a helping hand, or simply listening to their story, make a conscious effort to carry their burden alongside them.

Notes

Day 30: The Path to Triumph

Ali's Quote: "You're not going to enjoy every minute of the journey, but the success you'll find at the end will make it all worth it."

Scripture: "Blessed is the one who perseveres under trial because, having stood the test, that person will receive the crown of life that the Lord has promised to those who love him." - James 1:12

Prayer: Heavenly Father, help the reader persevere through difficult times, trusting that the reward will be worth it. Strengthen the reader's faith and resolve. Amen.

The Path to Triumph

As I sit here reflecting on my journey, I am reminded of the countless obstacles and trials I've faced. Each one felt insurmountable then, yet here I stand, a testament to the power of perseverance and faith. I want to share my story with you, not just to recount my experiences but to inspire you to find your strength and hope in the face of adversity.

There were days when the weight of my responsibilities felt like too much to bear. The expectations, the pressure to live up to my family name, and the relentless pursuit of my dreams often overwhelmed me. But it was during these moments of doubt and fatigue that I found my true strength.

I remember one particularly challenging period when everything seemed to be falling apart. My career was at a standstill, and I felt I was letting everyone down, including myself. I turned to my faith more than ever during this dark time. I clung to the promise in James 1:12, believing that if I could just endure, a crown of life would be waiting for me at the end of my trials.

I began to see each challenge not as a setback but as a stepping-stone. Every obstacle was an opportunity to grow stronger, learn, and become more resilient. I prayed for strength, for the ability to keep going even when the path was unclear. Slowly but surely, things began to change. Doors that had been firmly shut started to open, and new opportunities emerged.

One of the most important lessons I learned during this time was the power of perseverance. It's easy to give up when things get tough, but true success comes from pushing through those difficult moments. It's about having the faith to keep moving forward, even when you can't see the end in sight.

To anyone reading this who feels like they're at their breaking point, I want you to know that you are not alone. We all face trials, and we all have moments of doubt. But I promise you, if you keep going, hold on to your faith, and continue to persevere, you will find the success you seek. It may not come quickly, and it may not come easily, but it will come. And when it does, you'll look back and realize that every problematic moment was worth it.

Reflection: As we continue this 40-day journey, let us commit to carrying each other's burdens and fulfilling the law of Christ. Together, we can create a world where love and compassion reign and where everyone finds the strength to overcome their challenges.

Prophetic Word:

I believe you, reading this now, are on the brink of a breakthrough. The trials you face are not meant to break you but to build you. You have the strength to overcome and the perseverance to see your journey through to the end. Trust in God's plan for your life; know He is with you every step. Your victory is near, and the crown of life awaits you. Keep going, and do not lose heart.

Prayer: Heavenly Father, thank You for guiding us through our trials and for the promise of triumph that awaits us. As we continue this journey, help us to persevere with faith, knowing that You are refining us through each challenge. Strengthen our resolve and fill us with hope for the reward You have promised. May we carry each other's burdens, show love and compassion, and remain steadfast in pursuing Your will. Let us always trust that the success You have prepared for us will make the journey worthwhile. In Jesus' name, Amen.

Task: Reflect on the challenges you currently face and remind yourself that each trial is an opportunity for growth. Write down the challenges you face and the steps you can take to overcome them. Take one step at a time to move forward. Pray for strength and perseverance, and trust that each step brings you closer to your triumph. Trust that your persistence will be rewarded. Remember, the success you'll find will make it all worth it.

Notes

Day 31: The Journey to Recognizing Your Unique Worth

Ali's Quote: *"There are billions of people in the world, and every one of them is special. No one else in the world is like you."*

Scripture: *"I praise you because I am fearfully and wonderfully made; your works are wonderful; I know that full well."* - Psalm 139:14

Prayer: Heavenly Father, thank You for creating the reader uniquely and wonderfully. Help the reader to see the value in themselves and others, appreciating the diversity of Your creation. Amen.

The Journey to Recognizing Your Unique Worth

From the moment I could comprehend the world around me, I was captivated by the stories of the people I encountered. Each person, with their own dreams, struggles, and triumphs, was like a living book waiting to be read. I realized early on that no two stories were the same, each with unique beauty and significance.

Growing up, I often struggled with feeling different. As Muhammad Ali's nephew, I was placed under expectations and assumptions. People frequently saw me through the lens of my family's legacy, but I yearned to be seen for who I truly was. During these moments of introspection and prayer, I discovered the profound truth of Psalm 139:14. I was fearfully and wonderfully made, a unique creation of God, just like everyone else.

I remember a pivotal moment in my life that brought this realization to the forefront. It was a quiet evening, and I was sitting alone in my room, overwhelmed by the weight of expectations. I opened my Bible and read Psalm 139:14 repeatedly, letting the words sink into my soul. "I praise you because I am fearfully and wonderfully made; your works are wonderful; I know that full well." It was as if a light had been switched on inside me. I began to see myself not through the eyes of others but through the eyes of my Creator.

With this newfound perspective, I noticed the unique qualities that made me who I am. My compassion for others, ability to connect deeply with people, and unwavering faith were not just characteristics; they were gifts from God. And these gifts were meant to be shared with the world.

One day, while volunteering at a local shelter, I met a young man named James. He was quiet, reserved, and struggling with his sense of worth. We spent hours talking, and as he shared his story, I could see the pain and self-doubt in his eyes. I told him about my journey of self-discovery and how I had learned to see myself through God's eyes. I shared Psalm 139:14 with him and encouraged him to see the unique and wonderful person that he was.

Over time, James began to open up and embrace his uniqueness. He discovered a talent for painting, which became a powerful outlet for his emotions and a way to connect with others. Watching him transform from someone who felt invisible to someone who recognized his worth was a testament to the power of seeing oneself through the lens of God's love.

As you read this, I want you to know that you are also a unique and wonderful creation. There is no one else in the world like you. Embrace your individuality and let your light shine. Remember the words of Psalm 139:14 and let them remind you of your inherent worth.

Reflection: As you continue your 40-day journey to greatness, remember to reflect on the unique qualities that make you special. Write down three things you love about yourself and admire in others. Embrace the diversity in God's creation and celebrate the beauty of individuality.

Prophetic Word:

I speak over you today and say that you are not defined by the expectations of others or the challenges you face. You are defined by the love and purpose that God has placed within you. You are fearfully and wonderfully made; your unique gifts are meant to make a difference in this world. Stand firm in your identity, and let your life be a testament to the incredible power of God's creation.

> **Prayer:** Heavenly Father, thank You for reminding us of the beauty and worth You have placed in each of us. As we reflect on our unique qualities, help us to embrace our individuality and recognize the value You have given us. Open our hearts to appreciate the diversity in others and to celebrate the wonderful ways You have made each person. May we always walk confidently, knowing that we are fearfully and wonderfully made by Your hand. In Jesus' name, Amen.

Task: Today, reflect on the unique qualities that make you special. Write down three things you love about yourself and admire in others. Embrace the diversity in God's creation and celebrate the beauty of individuality.

Your journey is unique, and your impact is profound. Walk confidently, knowing you are a unique and irreplaceable part of God's magnificent creation.

BOOK TITLE

Notes

Day 32: Maintain Balance

Ali's Quote: "It isn't the mountains ahead to climb that wear you out; it's the pebble in your shoe."

Scripture: "There is a time for everything, and a season for every activity under the heavens." - Ecclesiastes 3:1

Prayer: Heavenly Father, help the reader to maintain balance in their life. May they find harmony in their work, rest, and relationships, trusting in Your perfect timing. Amen.

Maintaining Balance

Life often feels like a relentless climb, with towering mountains of responsibility and ambition constantly in view. Muhammad Ali once said, "It isn't the mountains ahead to climb that wear you out; it's the pebble in your shoe." This truth resonates deeply with me, Ibn Ali, because I've learned that it's not always the big challenges that drain us but the small, which are often overlooked obstacles that can derail our progress.

I recall a time in my life when I was intensely focused on achieving a significant goal. The path ahead seemed daunting, but I was determined to succeed. I trained harder than ever, pushing my body and mind to their limits.

Every day was a battle against the clock, squeezing in every ounce of effort to move closer to my dream. But as the days wore on, something subtle began to eat away at my resolve.

It wasn't the physical exhaustion or the weight of the goal itself that threatened to undo me; it was the little things—the minor irritations and neglected areas of my life. My relationships started to suffer as I became increasingly absorbed in my work. I ignored the need for rest, thinking I could push through the fatigue. The balance that once gave me strength was replaced by a single-minded pursuit that left me feeling hollow.

One evening, as I sat alone, drained and frustrated, I opened my Bible to Ecclesiastes 3:1: "There is a time for everything and a season for every activity under the heavens." These words hit me like a bolt of lightning. I realized that I had been so focused on the mountain ahead that I had ignored the pebble in my shoe—the imbalance in my life slowly wearing me down.

I knew I needed to make a change. I began to reassess how I was spending my time, carving out space for rest, for my loved ones, and moments of quiet reflection. It wasn't easy to shift gears, especially when the world around me seemed to glorify relentless hustle. However, I discovered that by maintaining balance, I preserved my energy and found greater clarity and purpose in my pursuits.

As I restored balance in my life, I noticed a remarkable difference in my performance and well-being. My relationships improved, my mind became sharper, and I approached my work with renewed passion. The pebble that had once caused so much discomfort was gone, and the climb up the mountain became smoother and more enjoyable.

Prophetic Word:

To you, the reader, I want to speak this into your life: The mountains you face may seem insurmountable, but do not let the small, unnoticed challenges steal your strength. Pay attention to the balance in your life, for it is in harmony that you will find the energy and wisdom to overcome the more significant obstacles. God has set a time for everything, and His timing is perfect. Trust in His plan, and allow yourself the grace to rest, to connect with others, and to seek His presence daily.

> **Prayer:** Heavenly Father, thank You for the wisdom to seek balance in our lives. As we reflect on the areas where we may be out of harmony, guide us to make the necessary adjustments that honor You and bring peace.

Help us to trust in Your perfect timing for every season of our lives, and may we find rest, strength, and fulfillment in balancing our work, relationships, and personal time. Keep us centered on You as we move forward. In Jesus' name, Amen.

Task: Take a moment today to evaluate your balance between work, rest, and personal time in life. Are you giving too much of yourself to one area while neglecting others? Seek to restore balance, trusting that God will guide you. Adjust your routine to ensure you nurture your body, mind, and spirit without neglecting any crucial areas. Remember, it's not just about reaching the summit but about enjoying the journey with peace and wholeness in your heart.

BOOK TITLE

Notes

Day 33: Reflect on the Journey

Ali's Quote: *"Float like a butterfly, sting like a bee. The hands can't hit what the eyes can't see."*

Scripture: *"Let us examine our ways and test them and let us return to the Lord."*
- Lamentations 3:40

Prayer: Heavenly Father, as the reader reflects on their journey, may they see Your hand guiding them every step of the way. Let this reflection bring them closer to You. Amen.

The Lesson in the Ring

The familiar scent of sweat and leather filled my senses as I stood in the gym. This place had become my second home, a sanctuary where I could channel all my energy, frustrations, and dreams. As I hit the heavy bag, it slightly swayed, each punch a reminder of the countless hours I had spent preparing for this moment. There was something different in the air today—a sense of anticipation mixed with doubt.

Growing up as Muhammad Ali's nephew, I was always surrounded by greatness. My uncle's words, "Float like a butterfly, sting like a bee. The hands can't hit what the eyes can't see," were ingrained in my mind as a mantra and a way of life. Yet, despite all the training and lessons passed down to me, I faced a challenge that tested everything I thought I knew.

I had been preparing for this fight for months, knowing my opponent was known for his speed and agility. He was the kind of fighter who could slip away from any punch, leaving his adversaries swinging at nothing but air. As I wrapped my hands, I couldn't help but think of the significance of this fight—not just as another step in my career but as a test of my resolve, patience, and understanding of the lessons I had learned.

When the fight began, it didn't take long for me to realize just how fast my opponent was. Every time I tried to land a punch, he was already gone, dancing around me with an ease that only heightened my frustration. I started to doubt myself, wondering if all those hours in the gym had been enough. Was I really prepared for this?

The bell rang, ending the first round, and I stumbled back to my corner, breathing heavily. My coach, a man who had seen it all, looked at me with calm eyes. "You're trying too hard to land the big punch," he said, his voice steady. "Remember, it's not just about power but strategy, timing, and focus. Float, don't force."

I nodded, but his words didn't fully resonate with me at that moment. When the second round started, I was back in the same frustrating cycle—

my opponent slipping away, me swinging at shadows. By the time the third round ended, I was physically and mentally exhausted. I felt like I was chasing something I couldn't catch, always one step behind.

As I sat in my corner, trying to catch my breath, a scripture my mother often quoted came to mind: "Let us examine our ways and test them, and let us return to the Lord" (Lamentations 3:40). It was a call to reflect, to reassess, to find my way back to the basics. In that moment of quiet desperation, I realized that this fight wasn't just about brute strength or speed; it was about something more profound. It was about understanding the real lesson I was meant to learn.

The fourth round began, and this time, I approached it differently. I slowed my pace, focusing not on the power of my punches but on my footwork, timing, and awareness. I began to see the patterns in my opponent's movements, the subtle shifts that hinted at where he would move next.

I started to float.

It was as if something clicked inside me. My movements became smoother and more deliberate. I wasn't just reacting; I was anticipating. And then, in a split second, I saw my opening. My opponent threw a punch, overextending just enough for me to counter. With precision, I landed a combination that sent him staggering back.

The crowd roared, but I stayed focused. This wasn't about the applause or the victory—it was about understanding the lesson in the struggle. The fight continued, and with each round, I grew more confident in my physical abilities and mental and spiritual strength. I finally understood that my uncle's famous words weren't just about the physical aspects of boxing; they were about the mindset, the wisdom to know when to strike and when to hold back, and the humility to learn and adapt.

When the final bell rang, and my hand was raised in victory, I felt a deep sense of satisfaction, not because I had won the fight but because I had learned a lesson that would stay with me for the rest of my life. I had learned to float like a butterfly and sting like a bee, not just with my fists but with my mind and spirit.

As I left the ring, I whispered a prayer of thanks, reflecting on the journey that had brought me to this point. The lessons learned in that ring were ones I would carry with me forever—lessons of patience, humility, and the importance of reflection.

Reflection: To you, my friend, I say this: Your journey will have its own battles, its own moments of doubt and frustration. But in those moments, remember to pause, reflect, and return to the basics. Examine your ways and let the lessons of your journey guide you. You have the strength within you, the wisdom to navigate the challenges ahead, and the humility to grow from them. And as you float through the challenges, remember that there is a time to sting, a time to rise above, and a time to claim victory—not just in the ring, but in life.

Prophetic Word on Reflection

As you take this time to reflect on your journey, the Lord is inviting you into a deeper understanding of His presence in every step you have taken. I hear the Lord saying, "Do not rush through this moment of reflection, for it is in the quiet and stillness that you will hear My voice most clearly. I have been with you from the beginning, guiding your every step, even in the moments when you could not see Me."

This reflection is a sacred space where God wants to reveal the lessons He has been teaching you, the growth you have experienced, and how He has molded your character. The Lord is saying, "Look back and see My faithfulness. I have carried you through the storms and have been your shelter in times of need."

As you examine your ways, as Lamentations 3:40 encourages, let it be a time of returning to the Lord with a renewed heart and mind. The Lord is calling you to let go of the past's burdens and mistakes, learn from them, and step forward into the future with a heart full of hope and trust in Him.

The Lord wants to remind you that your journey is not just about the destination but the transformation that has occurred along the way. Every challenge, every victory, and every lesson learned has been a part of His divine plan to shape you into the person you are today.

In this time of reflection, may you see God's hand in every chapter of your story. Let this reflection bring you closer to Him with a heart full of gratitude for all He has done and will continue to do in your life.

> **Prayer:** Heavenly Father, thank You for walking with us through this journey. As we reflect on where we've been and the lessons we've learned, help us see Your guiding hand in every moment. May this reflection draw us closer to You, deepening our trust in Your plan for our lives. Strengthen our hearts as we continue carrying the wisdom You've given us. In Jesus' name, Amen.

Task: Spend time today reflecting on your entire journey. Are you swinging mindlessly or taking the time to understand the more profound lessons? Spend time examining your ways, testing them, and returning to the principles that guide you. Write down the key lessons you've learned and let them help you float through the challenges you face with the strength to sting when the time is right.

BOOK TITLE

Notes

Day 34: A Journey to Joy

Ali's Quote: *"I've seen George Foreman shadowboxing, and the shadow won."*

Scripture: *"A cheerful heart is good medicine, but a crushed spirit dries up the bones."* - Proverbs 17:22

Prayer: Heavenly Father, grant the reader a heart full of joy and laughter. Help the reader find humor in life's moments and share it with others. Amen.

A Journey to Joy

When I was young, I remember hearing my uncle, Muhammad Ali, tell the story about George Foreman's shadowboxing and how the shadow won. It was a funny line, a playful jab, but more than that, it held a more profound truth. Life has a way of shadowboxing us, throwing punches that we sometimes don't see coming. But in those moments, when we're up against the ropes, our spirit and attitude make all the difference.

One particular moment in my life stands out vividly. It was a time when everything seemed to be going wrong. Business was slow, personal challenges were piling up, and I felt like I was in a ring with life, taking hits left and right. My spirit was crushed, and I could feel the weight of it drying up my bones, just as Proverbs 17:22 warns.

But then I remembered my uncle's words and the laughter that followed them. I decided to find the humor in my situation. It wasn't easy at first, but I started to look for the small, funny moments in my day. The way my dog would chase its tail endlessly, and a friend would tell a joke and laugh harder than anyone else at it. These moments were my medicine, lifting my spirit and bringing a smile to my face.

One day, while struggling with some paperwork, I looked at my reflection in the mirror and imagined myself shadowboxing. I threw a few punches, made some exaggerated moves, and before I knew it, I was laughing at myself. That laughter was like a release, a way to let go of the stress and pressure that had been building up. It didn't solve all my problems but it gave me the strength to face them with a renewed spirit.

As the days passed, I continued to find joy in the little things. I reached out to friends and family, sharing my laughter and encouraging them to do the same. I realized that a cheerful heart truly is good medicine, not just for me but for everyone around me. My challenges didn't disappear, but my attitude towards them changed. I was no longer shadowboxing in the dark but dancing in the light.

To you, dear reader, I say this: Life will throw punches, and sometimes it will feel like you're losing to your own shadow. But remember that a cheerful heart is your greatest ally. Find humor in your day, no matter how small, and let it be your medicine. Share your laughter with others, and you'll find that your spirit will lift, and so will theirs.

Prophetic Word:

I see you standing firm, a beacon of joy and resilience. The shadows in your life may loom large, but they will not overcome you. You are destined to rise above them, to find laughter amid trials, and to inspire others with your cheerful heart. The joy you cultivate today will be the strength you draw upon tomorrow. Embrace it, share it, and watch as it transforms not only your life but the lives of those around you.

In this journey, may you always find a reason to smile, a reason to laugh, and a reason to hope. Your cheerful heart will be your greatest weapon, your most powerful ally. Let it guide, heal, and lift you to new heights.

So, take this call to action to heart. Find your joy, live it out, and be a light source for others. And always remember, no matter how tough the fight, you have the strength to overcome.

> **Prayer:** Heavenly Father, thank You for the gift of joy and laughter that lifts our spirits and brings healing to our hearts. As we walk through life's good and challenging moments, help us find joy in every season. Let our laughter be a reflection of Your love and a source of strength for ourselves and those around us. Fill our hearts with cheer, and may we spread Your light wherever we go. In Jesus' name, Amen.

Task: Today, seek out moments of joy and share laughter with someone else. Whether through a conversation, a funny story, or simply appreciating life's lighter moments, allow joy to fill your heart and spread to those around you.

Notes

Day 35: Striving for Greatness

Ali's Quote: *"To make America the greatest is my goal, so I beat the Russian, and I beat the Pole. And for the U.S.A. won the medal of gold. The Greeks said, 'You're better than the Cassius of old.'"*

Scripture: *"Do you not know that in a race, all the runners run, but only one gets the prize? Run in such a way as to get the prize."* - 1 Corinthians 9:24

Prayer: Heavenly Father, help the reader to strive for excellence in all they do, running the race with determination and integrity. Let the reader's efforts bring honor to You and the community. Amen.

Striving for Greatness

Reflecting on my journey, I'm reminded of the intense training, the sacrifices, and the unwavering determination that led me to victory. The path was difficult, filled with challenges that tested my resolve and strength. But each step and struggle brought me closer to my goal: to bring honor to my country and uphold the legacy of greatness.

My story begins with a dream, a vision to achieve something remarkable. Inspired by my uncle, Muhammad Ali, I knew that greatness wasn't just about physical prowess but about the spirit and heart behind every action. It was about fighting for something bigger than oneself, a cause that would inspire others to rise above their circumstances.

The journey to the top was arduous. I faced opponents who were not only skilled but also hungry for victory. Each match was a test of my skill, strategy, and endurance. But I knew that the actual battle was within me. It was about overcoming self-doubt, pushing beyond limits, and believing in the impossible.

One particular match stands out in my memory. It was against a formidable Russian boxer known for his relentless aggression and unmatched strength. As I stood in the ring, the weight of expectations and the fear of failure loomed over me. But in that moment, I remembered the words of the scripture: "Run in such a way as to get the prize." It wasn't just about winning but giving my all and fighting with integrity and determination.

The match was intense, each round pushing me to my limits. But with every punch, I felt a surge of strength, not just from my physical training but from a deeper source of power. I could feel the presence of God guiding me and giving me the courage to press on. When the final bell rang, and my hand was raised in victory, I knew it was more than a win. It was a testament to the power of faith, perseverance, and the unyielding spirit to overcome.

But the journey didn't end there. Every victory brought new challenges and new mountains to climb. I continued to train and push myself, always striving for excellence. And in every challenge, I found an opportunity to grow, learn, and inspire others. I realized that greatness wasn't just about the medals or the accolades; it was about the impact I could make in the lives of others.

Through my journey, I have encountered many who are struggling and facing their own battles. To them, I say: never give up. No matter how tough the road or how insurmountable the obstacles may seem, there is always hope. Draw strength from your faith, believe in your dreams, and keep pushing forward. Your journey may be difficult, but it is in those moments of struggle that true greatness is forged.

Prophetic Word:

I declare that you are destined for greatness. To everyone reading this, God has a unique purpose and plan for your life. Your past or your failures do not define you. Instead, you are shaped by your resilience, faith, and determination to overcome. Embrace the journey, run the race with endurance, and you will see the incredible things God has in store for you.

>**Prayer:** Heavenly Father, thank You for calling us to strive for greatness in all we do. As we run the race You have set before us, help us to pursue excellence with determination and integrity. May our efforts reflect Your glory and bring honor to those around us. Strengthen our resolve to keep pushing forward and guide us to achieve the purpose You've placed in our hearts. In Jesus' name, Amen.

Task: Reflect on your goals and dreams. What are the challenges you are facing? How can you draw strength from your faith and your inner resolve to overcome them? Take a moment to pray, seek guidance, and commit to running your race with determination and integrity. Remember, you are not alone in this journey. With God by your side, you can achieve greatness.

BOOK TITLE

Notes

Week 6: Finish Strong

Day 36: A Journey of Identity and Strength

Ali's Quote: *"The name Muhammad is the most common name in the world. In all the countries around the world—Pakistan, Saudi Arabia, Morocco, Turkey, Syria, Lebanon—there are more Muhammads than anything else. When I joined the Nation of Islam and became a Muslim, they gave me the most famous name because I was the champ."*

Scripture: *"But now, this is what the Lord says—he who created you, Jacob, he who formed you, Israel: 'Do not fear, for I have redeemed you; I have summoned you by name; you are mine.'"* - Isaiah 43:1

Prayer: Heavenly Father, thank You for calling the reader by name and making them Yours. Help the reader to live up to the name You have given them and to honor You in all they do. Amen.

A Journey of Identity and Strength

When I reflect on the name Muhammad, I'm reminded of its powerful legacy. This name, held by millions worldwide, speaks of strength, faith, and perseverance. It's a name that reminds me of my journey, which started long before I understood its full significance.

I remember the day I took on the name Muhammad. It wasn't just a change of identity but a transformation of purpose. I had to live up to the legacy of not just being the nephew of Muhammad Ali but of carrying a name that millions look up to. It was both an honor and a challenge, a calling to rise above the ordinary and step into a greater destiny.

Life has thrown many challenges my way. There were moments when I felt the weight of expectations, the pressure to perform, and the fear of failure. But in those moments, I found strength in knowing I was not alone. Just as God spoke through the prophet Isaiah, reminding Israel of their divine identity and redemption, I was reminded of my own.

Isaiah 43:1 has been a source of comfort and strength for me. "Do not fear, for I have redeemed you; I have summoned you by name; you are mine." These words are a powerful reminder that we are not defined by our struggles but by the One who calls us by name. It's a reminder that our identity is rooted in something greater than ourselves.

In my journey, I have learned that names carry power. They carry the weight of history, the hopes of the future, and our essence. When God calls us by name, He speaks to our deepest identity, our true self. He calls us to rise, to overcome, and to live victoriously.

One pivotal moment in my journey was when I faced a significant setback in my career. It felt like everything was crumbling around me, and I questioned my purpose. During that time, I turned to prayer and reflection. I sought God's guidance and asked for the strength to continue. In those quiet moments of prayer, I felt a profound sense of peace and reassurance. God reminded me that I was His, that my identity was secure in Him, and that He had a purpose for my life.

I realized that my setbacks were not the end of my story. They were merely chapters in a much larger narrative that God was writing. Each challenge was an opportunity to grow, learn, and become stronger. I learned to see my struggles not as obstacles but as stepping-stones toward my destiny.

Prophetic Word:

In this season, the Lord is speaking directly to your heart about your identity and the strength that comes from knowing who you are in Him. I hear the Lord saying, "You are not defined by your circumstances, nor by the names the world has tried to place upon you. You are defined by the name I have given you, which speaks of your true identity in Me."

God wants to remind you that your identity is rooted in Him alone. Just as He called Israel by name and reminded them of their divine identity, so is He calling you to embrace who you are in Him. The Lord says, "You are My beloved child, called by My name, and I have set you apart for a purpose." Do not fear the challenges that lie ahead, for they are merely opportunities to discover the strength I have placed within you.

Your strength comes not from your abilities but from the One who has redeemed you and called you by name. The Lord is your source of strength, your fortress in times of trouble. He is equipping you with everything you need to fulfill the destiny He has set before you. Remember, His power is made perfect in your weakness, and His grace is sufficient for every trial.

God is calling you to arise, to step boldly into the identity He has given you. He is breaking off the enemy's lies that have tried to hold you back and releasing you into a new season of confidence and strength. Stand firm in knowing that you are His, and nothing can separate you from His love.

As you walk in this truth, you will find that the strength you need is already within you, placed there by the Creator Himself. Embrace your identity in Christ, and let His strength carry you through every challenge.

Prayer: Heavenly Father, thank You for the identity You have given us and for calling us by name as Your own. Help us to walk confidently in the strength and purpose You have placed within us. May we live each day honoring the name You've given us, reflecting Your love and truth in all we do. Guide us as we continue this journey, and let our lives bring glory to Your name. In Jesus' name, Amen.

Task: Take a moment today to reflect on your journey. Write down the challenges you have faced and how they have shaped you. Remember that God has called you by name and has a purpose for your life. Embrace your identity in Him and step boldly into your destiny.

BOOK TITLE

Notes

Day 37: Believing in the Possible

Ali's Quote: *"If my mind can conceive it, and my heart can believe it—then I can achieve it."*

Scripture: *"'If you can?' said Jesus. 'Everything is possible for one who believes."* - Mark 9:23

Prayer: Heavenly Father, help the reader to believe in the possibilities You have set before them. Strengthen the reader's faith and guide their actions to achieve Your will. Amen.

The Power of Belief

Ibn Ali, Muhammad Ali's nephew, grew up surrounded by the idea of greatness. My uncle, Muhammad Ali, was an icon known worldwide, but what often went unnoticed was the depth of his belief in himself and his purpose. This belief didn't come from his physical prowess alone; it was a profound conviction that he was destined for greatness, instilled in him by his unwavering faith and determination.

One of the most pivotal moments in my life came when I faced an insurmountable challenge. I was preparing for a major boxing match that would determine the course of my career. Doubts crept in, and fear threatened to paralyze me. In those moments of doubt, I remembered the quote that had always guided me: "If my mind can conceive it, and my heart can believe it—then I can achieve it."

I turned to scripture for strength, and Mark 9:23 stood out: "'If you can?' said Jesus. 'Everything is possible for one who believes.'" This passage resonated deeply with me. It reminded me that belief isn't just a passive feeling; it's an active force that propels us toward our goals.

As I trained for the fight, I realized my journey wasn't just about winning a match. It was about proving to myself and others that with faith and determination, anything is possible. I visualized my victory every day. I saw myself standing in the ring, my hand raised in triumph. I felt the adrenaline, the crowd's roar, and the overwhelming sense of accomplishment. My mind conceived it, and my heart believed it.

On the day of the match, I walked into the ring with a sense of calm confidence. Every punch and move was driven by the belief that I could achieve what I had set out to do. And when the final bell rang, I stood victorious. It wasn't just a physical victory; it was a testament to the power of belief.

This journey taught me that obstacles are merely opportunities in disguise. They test our resolve and strengthen our faith. When we believe in the possibilities God has set before us, we tap into a source of strength far more significant than our own.

Prophetic Word for the Reader:

To you, dear reader, I say this: You have the power to overcome any challenge within you. The dreams and visions planted in your heart are there for a reason. They are your guiding stars, leading you toward your purpose. Believe in them. Nurture them with faith and action.

When doubt creeps in, remember the words of Jesus: "Everything is possible for one who believes." Your belief is a powerful force that can turn the impossible into the possible. Trust in God's plan for your life. He has equipped you with everything you need to succeed.

As you embark on this 40-day journey, let each day be a step toward realizing your dreams. Face each challenge with unwavering faith, knowing that you are not alone. God is with you, guiding you and strengthening you.

> **Prayer:** Heavenly Father, help us to believe in the possibilities You have set before us. Strengthen our faith and guide our actions to achieve Your will. Amen.

Task: Today, take a step toward your dreams. Write down your vision, pray over it, and take one action that moves you closer to achieving it. Believe that with God, all things are possible. Believe in the vision God has given you. Act on it with faith and determination.

Notes

Day 38: The Gift of Friendship

Ali's Quote: *"Friendship is not something you learn in school. But if you haven't learned the meaning of friendship, you really haven't learned anything."*

Scripture: *"A friend loves at all times, and a brother is born for a time of adversity."* - Proverbs 17:17

Prayer: Heavenly Father, thank You for the gift of friendship. Help the reader to be a true friend who loves at all times and supports others in their times of need. Amen.

Accept the Divine Covenant of Friendship

Growing up as Muhammad Ali's nephew, I was often surrounded by people who admired my uncle for his strength, charisma, and unwavering determination. However, one of the most valuable lessons I learned from him was the importance of true friendship.

There was a time when I found myself in the midst of a challenging season. It felt like the world was against me, and I was navigating the storm alone. My uncle's words echoed in my mind, "Friendship is not something you learn in school. But if you haven't learned the meaning of friendship, you really haven't learned anything."

One evening, as I sat alone in my room, feeling the weight of the world on my shoulders, I received a call from an old friend. His voice was warm and reassuring, a beacon of light in my darkness. He didn't have all the answers, but his presence reminded me I wasn't alone. He listened to my fears, encouraged me, and shared stories of our past adventures, making me laugh and momentarily forget my troubles.

Through his unwavering support, this friend taught me the true meaning of friendship. He showed me that a friend loves at all times and a brother is born for a time of adversity, just as Proverbs 17:17 tells us. His friendship was a testament to the power of love and support, especially during life's most challenging moments.

As days turned into weeks, my situation began to improve. I realized that my friend's support had been a lifeline, pulling me out of my despair and giving me the strength to persevere. His friendship was a divine gift, a reminder of God's love and provision.
Now, as I reflect on that time, I am grateful for the friends in my life. I understand that true friendship is not only being there when it's convenient but also standing by each other through thick and thin. It's about loving at all times and being a source of strength in times of adversity.

To you, dear reader, I offer this prophetic word: You are not alone. God has placed people in your life to support and uplift you. Open your heart to the friends around you and be the friend others need. In doing so, you will find strength, hope, and the courage to overcome any challenge.

Remember, friendship is a powerful gift from God. Cherish, nurture, and let it be a source of encouragement and inspiration in your journey. Reach out to your friends today and let them know how much they mean to you. Be a beacon of love and support, just as my friend was to me. Together, we can face adversity and emerge stronger, knowing we are loved and supported.

Prophetic Word on Friendship

In this moment, I sense that God is highlighting the importance of genuine, heartfelt friendships in your life. The Lord wants to remind you that you are not called to walk this journey alone. He has placed people around you, divine connections, who will stand with you in both the highs and the lows. These friendships are not by accident; God Himself orchestrates them to be a source of strength, comfort, and wisdom in your life.

I hear the Lord saying, "Cherish these relationships, for they are my gift to you. In times of trial, they will be your support; in times of joy, they will celebrate with you." Just as iron sharpens iron, God is using these friendships to refine you, to mold you into the person He has destined you to be. Allow yourself to be vulnerable, to open up, and to receive the love and support of those He has placed in your life.

The Lord also encourages you to be that friend who stands in the gap for others, to be a reflection of His love and faithfulness. As you sow into these relationships with kindness, patience, and understanding, you will reap a harvest of lasting, godly friendships that will carry you through all seasons.

Remember, true friendship is a covenant relationship mirroring the love Christ has for us. Embrace these divine connections and allow them to flourish, for you will find the strength to face whatever comes your way.

> **Prayer:** Heavenly Father, thank You for the precious gift of friendship. We are grateful for the friends You've placed in our lives, who stand by us in joy and adversity. Help us to be faithful friends who love, support, and encourage others just as You have called us to. Teach us to cherish and nurture these relationships, reflecting Your love through our actions. In Jesus' name, Amen.

Task: Reflect on the friends in your life. Reach out to someone today, offering your support and love. Commit to being a friend who stands by others in good and bad times.

Notes

Day 39: Mapping Change

Ali's Quote: *"Wars of nations are fought to change maps. But wars of poverty are fought to map change."*

Scripture: *"The King will reply, 'Truly I tell you, whatever you did for one of the least of these brothers and sisters of mine, you did for me."* - Matthew 25:40

Prayer: Heavenly Father, open the reader's heart to serve those in need and to fight against poverty and injustice. Help the reader to see every act of kindness as serving You. Amen

Mapping Change: Jesus' Word

I remember a time when the words of Jesus in Matthew 25:40 resonated deeply within my soul. It was a period in my life when I was surrounded by people facing insurmountable challenges, struggling to make ends meet, and losing hope. As Muhammad Ali's nephew, I carry a legacy of fighting in the ring and in life. And this fight, I realized, wasn't just about physical strength but about the strength of character, spirit, and faith.

One day, I walked through a neighborhood ravaged by poverty. The streets were lined with abandoned homes, children playing with makeshift toys, and adults worn down by the weight of their circumstances. The air was thick with despair, and I felt a stirring in my heart—a call to action, a call to serve.

As I moved deeper into the neighborhood, I met a young boy named David. His eyes, though weary, held a spark of hope. He told me about his dreams of becoming an engineer and desiring to build things that would improve his community. But the harsh reality of his situation overshadowed his dreams—his family could barely afford basic necessities, let alone educational resources.

Inspired by David's resilience, I decided to help. I connected him with local resources, provided him with books, and even arranged for a mentor who could guide him in his studies. Over time, David's grades improved, and his confidence grew. He began to see his dreams as attainable goals, not just distant fantasies.

In helping David, I saw firsthand the power of fighting the war against poverty. It wasn't about grand gestures but small, consistent acts of kindness and support. No matter how insignificant it seemed, each action contributed to mapping change in David's life and, by extension, the lives of those around him.

This experience taught me that every one of us has the power to be a catalyst for change. We don't need all the resources in the world; we need a willing heart and the determination to make a difference. When we fight against poverty, we aren't just altering maps; we are mapping out new paths for a future filled with hope, opportunity, and transformation.

As you embark on this 40-day journey, I encourage you to look around and find your own David. It could be a neighbor, a colleague, or even a stranger you meet on the street. Extend a helping hand, offer a word of encouragement, and let your actions reflect the love of Christ. Remember, the smallest act of kindness can ignite the brightest flame of hope.

Prophetic Word:

To every reader, I speak this prophetic word over you: You are a beacon of light in a world that often seems dark. Your acts of kindness, no matter how small, are seeds planted in fertile soil. God sees your heart and your willingness to serve. As you step out in faith and compassion, He will multiply your efforts, bringing forth a harvest of blessings. Do not grow weary in doing good, for in due season, you will reap if you do not give up. The changes you help map today will lead to a brighter future for future generations.

Stay strong, stay faithful, and keep fighting the good fight.

> **Prayer:** Heavenly Father, thank You for calling us to be agents of change in a world filled with need. As we serve others, help us to see each act of kindness as a reflection of Your love and a step toward justice. Open our hearts to the struggles of those around us and give us the courage to stand against poverty and injustice. May our actions bring light to those in darkness and create ripples of lasting change. In Jesus' name, Amen.

Task: Today, let us commit to being a light in someone's darkness. Reach out to someone in need, offer a helping hand, and let your actions reflect the love of Christ. Every small act can create ripples of change.

Notes

Day 40: Help People

Ali's Quote: *"The more we help others, the more we help ourselves."*

Scripture: *"Carry each other's burdens, and in this way, you will fulfill the law of Christ."* - Galatians 6:2

Prayer: Heavenly Father, teach the reader to serve others selflessly and to find joy in helping those in need. May my actions reflect Your love and compassion. Amen.

Help People

I remember the day clearly. It was a cold, rainy afternoon, and I was walking down a busy street, lost in my own thoughts. Life had been throwing curveballs at me left and right, and I felt overwhelmed by my challenges. As I trudged along, head down, I noticed a homeless man sitting on the sidewalk, shivering and drenched. He had a sign that read, "Need Help. God Bless."

Something stirred within me. Despite my own troubles, I felt a strong urge to help the man. I approached him and asked if he needed anything. He looked up at me with tired eyes and said, "I could really use a warm meal." Without hesitation, I took him to a nearby diner and bought him a hot meal. We sat together and talked while he ate. He shared his story, and I listened, offering words of encouragement and hope.

As we parted ways, I felt a sense of fulfillment I hadn't felt in a long time. Despite my struggles, helping the man lifted my spirits. Then, I realized the truth of the quote: "The more we help others, the more we help ourselves."

From that day forward, I made it a point to look for opportunities to help others, no matter how small the act. Whether volunteering at a local shelter, lending a listening ear to a friend in need, or simply offering a smile to a stranger, I found that each act of kindness helped others and strengthened me.

One experience stands out. I was volunteering at a community center when I met a young woman named Sarah. She was a single mother, struggling to make ends meet while caring for her two young children. Her face was etched with worry, and her eyes reflected the weight of her burdens. I spent time talking with her, offering support and resources to help her get back on her feet.

Over the weeks that followed, I saw a transformation in Sarah. With the help she received, she found a job and a stable place to live. Her children thrived, and her smile returned. Witnessing her journey from despair to hope was incredibly rewarding. It reinforced my belief that helping others impacts their lives and brings us immense joy and purpose.

My journey of helping others taught me valuable lessons. I learned that we all have the power to make a difference, no matter how small our actions may seem. I realized that in lifting others, we rise as well. Each act of kindness, each moment of compassion, creates a ripple effect that can change lives, including our own.

Prophetic Word:

To you, dear reader, I want to share a prophetic word. You are called to be a beacon of light in a world that often seems dark. Your struggles and challenges are not in vain; they are preparing you for a greater purpose. As you step out in faith to help others, you will find strength and healing in your own life. God has placed within you the ability to bring hope and transformation to those around you. Trust in His plan and know that your efforts to serve others will be blessed abundantly.

Prayer: Heavenly Father, thank You for our journey together, learning to serve and uplift those around us. As we continue forward, help us to carry the burdens of others with love and compassion, reflecting the heart of Christ in all we do. Fill us with a selfless spirit, finding joy in helping those in need. May our lives be a testimony of Your grace and love, and may we always seek to serve You by serving others. In Jesus' name, Amen.

Task: Today, I challenge you to look beyond your own circumstances and find someone you can help. It could be a friend, a neighbor, or even a stranger. Offer a kind word, lend a helping hand, or listen with an open heart. As you carry the burdens of others, you will fulfill the law of Christ and experience the true joy and fulfillment that comes from serving selflessly.

May your journey be filled with opportunities to bless others, and may you find strength, hope, and joy in every act of kindness you offer. Remember, the more we help others, the more we help ourselves.

May you seek God's approval above all else and find peace in knowing that His opinion is the one that truly matters. As you take this first step on your journey, I pray that you let go of any fear or doubt, trusting that God is with you every step of the way, guiding and transforming you.
Remember, you are free—free to be a servant of Christ, free to walk in the light of His truth, and free to live out the purpose He has placed on your life.

Notes

Conclusion:

Reflecting on my 40-day journey, the transformation from sinner to saint feels more tangible than ever. These past days have been filled with challenges, self-discovery, and profound moments of clarity. Through each step, I've come to understand that true transformation isn't about perfection; it's about surrender. It's about acknowledging our flaws and sins and then stepping into the light, embracing the grace freely offered us.

A powerful truth has become the cornerstone of my transformation: **From sinner to saint is only a decision away.** We must make this decision daily—to turn away from what holds us back and step boldly into the life that God has called us to. This decision isn't about earning God's love or approval but accepting it despite our shortcomings.

We are all sinners who fall short of God's glory, yet we are all offered the same invitation—to be transformed by His love and renewed by His grace. As I've walked through these 40 days, I've realized that this transformation is less about grand gestures and more about small, daily choices to live in alignment with God's will, serve others, and reflect Christ's love.

To you, dear reader, I offer this encouragement: Your journey is unique, but the opportunity for transformation is universal. No matter where you are today or what sins weigh heavy on your heart, know that you are only a decision away from stepping into the life of a saint. It begins with a single act of surrender, a simple prayer, a humble confession that opens the door to God's abundant grace.

As you go forward, remember that we are all in this together. None of us are perfect, but each of us is perfectly loved by the One who can transform our lives. Let this truth guide, strengthen, and inspire you as you continue your journey. May your days ahead be filled with the courage to make that daily decision, the wisdom to seek God's will, and the grace to embrace the saint within you.

From sinner to saint is only a decision away—make that decision today and watch as God begins to work wonders in your life.

Ministry websites:

Sinner &. Saint, The Kingdom Fight with Tom Renz
Www.thekingdomfight.org
Sinner and Saint podcast with Tom Renz
Rumble.com @ Sinner and Saint Podcast

Kingdom Jewelz with Joe Dingle
Rumble.com @ Joe Dingle

FreedomBrigades
Rumble.com @ FreedomBrigades

Floyd Martin
ATAP ministries with Floyd Martin
http://atapwithgod.com/
https://atapllc.net/ministries/
https://atapllc.net/about-us/

Seven Daughters of OM Publishing
https://sevendaughtersofom.tv
publishing@sevendaughtersofom.tv

www.ingramcontent.com/pod-product-compliance
Lightning Source LLC
Chambersburg PA
CBHW060503090426
42735CB00011B/2090